1any of us in Marysville have been grou
nce *We Are Absolutely Not Okay* made i
ves; they have given our students hope ᴜ
hat has happened to them. They have shown that sharing your story can truly set
ou free.
                    —*Jaci LeGore-Hodgins, teacher and coach, Marysville Getchell High School*

ᴜs a legislator, I know that we make better decisions when we stop, take a moment,
nd listen. Listen to the voices that offer a unique perspective, listen to the voices that
ɾe honest and come from the heart. Listen to the voices that aren't always heard.
hrough the writings of these Scriber Lake students we hear those voices, and I, for
ne, will make better decisions because of it.
                    —*State Representative Strom Peterson, 21st Legislative District*

hese writers have been told stories about who they are and what they can be, and
ow they have the chance to change the narrative and write their own stories—both
f their pasts and for their futures. This kind of self-awareness and vulnerability is
hat the world needs right now.
                    —*Jessica McCarthy, nonprofit consultant, Seattle*

tudents need the opportunity to share their experiences, and this opportunity does
ist that. The ability to open up and express their inner thoughts, challenges, and
ictories in a student-first voice is critical to understanding how it is to be a young
erson in this ever-changing world.
                    —*Dr. Gustavo Balderas, Superintendent, Edmonds School District*

Vith each story, these student authors invite us into their lives. Accept this invitation.
isten to their lives. Hear each soul screaming to be heard.
                    —*Jeff Stone, Social Studies and Ethnic Studies Lead, Edmonds School District*

ⱸedicine for what ails us these days? Try a shot of resilience and perseverance,
ourtesy of the inspiring accounts put forth by these gifted writers. Inspiring, indeed.
—*Chris Brown (not the rapper), Outdoor Education Teacher, Scriber Lake High School*

criber students draw you into their personal experiences with outstanding detail,
hen inspire you with resilient self-reflection. Their process allows us to reflect on
ur own struggles as young adults.
                    —*Mark Stewart, teacher and coach, Mariner High School;*
                    Husky legend, University of Washington

ᴮold. Brave. Determined. These gripping stories reveal the souls of young lives next
ɪoor, of those whom we might not otherwise know. Through storytelling, these
ourneys of sadness, rage, and resiliency unfold before our eyes. As these young
vriters reclaim their voices, we gain renewed hope in our community.
                    —*Kurt and Anne Kutay, Edmonds residents and Scriber super-fans*

this
SMILE is for
EVERYONE
else

this
SMILE is for
EVERYONE
else

edited by
Marjie Bowker
Leighanne Law

STEEP STAIRS PRESS
Edmonds, Washington

Published by
Steep Stairs Press
23200 100th Ave W
Edmonds, WA 98020
425.431.7270
steepstairspress.com
facebook.com/steepstairspress

Cover art by
Stephanie Souza

Copyedited and designed by
Tim Holsopple
Armored Bear Design + Detail
armoredbear.cc

Photo of *the* steep stairs by
Tim Holsopple

LCCN
2021908025

ISBN
978-0-9974724-3-1

BOOKS PUBLISHED BY
STEEP STAIRS PRESS

To Bob Fuller and George Murray,
champions since the beginning.

TABLE OF CONTENTS

EDITORS' NOTE

It's inevitable: a new Scriber book brings new endeavors and refreshed resources.

The pandemic created an opportunity for us to move in a new direction: into the student-produced podcast world. We now have a Steep Stairs Podcast class producing episodes featuring our writers' stories and surrounding themes, and the resulting podcasts are available on several major platforms. Our primary platform is YouTube; the QR code and corresponding link to the Steep Stairs Press YouTube channel appear at the end of each story in this book. Check back often as more content is added. See the introduction to the Steep Stairs Podcast in the Resources section for more information.

The further reading resource, Bibliotherapy and the Scriber Books, has been updated for this volume. Leighanne Law compiled the original list for our 2019 book, and Rachel Ramey has added new books of interest.

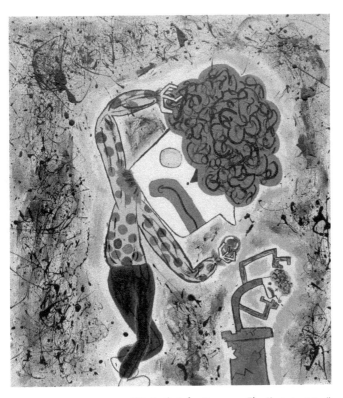

This Smile Is for Everyone Else (featuring Nigel)
Stephanie Souza
2020

INTRODUCTION

Marjie Bowker

Stephanie Souza's painting of a big clown modeling behavior for a little clown was chosen as the front cover by this volume's writers in February 2020.

The painting had been displayed in my classroom for over a year by then—along with more than twenty-five other works of Stephanie's. But the clowns always drew the most attention. One student who lingered in front of it for a long time finally said, "This was me before coming to Scriber. I was trying to do what everyone told me I was supposed to do." Another said, simply, "I feel that."

The image definitely works as a representation of the stories in this book. Each writer was attempting to navigate the educational system while dealing with all kinds of trauma: abuse, poverty, addiction, and abandonment. They tried to do things the way they had been told—they were the little clowns who had learned to "put on a face" for everyone else—until they just couldn't do it that way anymore. Until they felt like shadows of who they were meant to be.

Then they landed at Scriber. Gradually, they began to peel away layers, accept themselves, and discover other ways forward. Eventually, each one made the choice to use writing as an outlet to cope with the past and present, and as a doorway to enter a more hopeful, authentic future.

Ironically, they were deep into the process of writing toward metaphorical mask removal when the world shut down and masked up—just one month after they made the prescient cover decision. And, despite the confusion of an online school format and various pandemic traumas, they continued to work on their stories through Zoom conferencing and Google Docs. They didn't do this for a grade—grades were no one's focus during the spring of 2020. They did it because they had a purpose.

Now that it is June 2021 and we are on the "other side" in many ways—the other side of the pandemic, the other side of unpacking these stories—the painting offers another perspective: perhaps the big clown is actually taking the mask *off*, and modeling *that* behavior for the little clown. In this interpretation, anyone who has ever had the courage to be painfully honest, become unbelievably vulnerable, and then find their own way forward can model that courageous message for others.

Over the past ten years, more than 120 students have written their way toward more self-knowledge through this program. In 2011, Scriber students began writing what would become our first book, *We Are Absolutely Not Okay*. Our message now is the same as it was laid out in the first introduction: "If you have ever felt alone, betrayed, confused, or angry, this book is for you. If you have ever come to school pretending everything is okay when really everything is absolutely not, we want you to know that there is hope—even in the darkest situations. We are real and our stories are real, so you need not feel alone with your struggles."

Being seen, heard, and known is the most exhilarating kind of freedom to experience. And, we believe, it leads to the most authentic kind of smiling.

for EVERYONE else

Twisted Mind
Stephanie Souza
2019

I GOT THE FEELING

Thalia Sykes

"Look at that stupid bitch," I hear coming from behind me as I put my math book in the crate. "I hate that she's in this class."

I know this voice. It's Melissa's, and it's been a week since I decided to stop talking to her and her friends, who huddle around her, giggling at her words.

I came to this small-town school a few months ago and was just becoming comfortable, starting to find my place, when I realized what my other new acquaintances were telling me was true: Melissa was a monster, a bully. She began to give me dirty looks when I stopped having lunch with her and started reading instead. I have already seen the way she deals with people she doesn't like, so I know she isn't going to stop there. I know she is a snake about to strike.

When the bell rings, the tension builds. *Something's going to happen.* I step outside the classroom and feel five pairs of eyes burning holes into the back of my head. They're following me. I sense Melissa is about to spew acid my way, and my stomach becomes a ball of nerves.

"Nigger," she says.

I can feel the bile bubbling up in my throat.

Then, one by one, her four minions follow her lead and the word becomes a chant.

"Nigger, nigger, nigger!"

The word pounds in my ears. My face burns and I'm instantly sweating all over. I turn and lock eyes with one of her sidekicks, his eyes black with anger. I see the dirt under his nails and the yellow on his teeth. The smirk on his cherub-cheeked face makes it look like he's having fun. In fact, all of them are filled with smiles and glee. Except for Melissa.

She wears a twisted grin that spells out "I hate you" and "Are you sorry now?"

"You're a fucking fat elephant nigger!" she spits. Fear overtakes my mind, and all I want to do is shrink down and disappear.

I pick up my pace to escape the acid that is now all over me. As I run away from them—my skin burning—I truly feel like the fat elephant she says I am. I look down and see thick, gray legs and calves. I feel the ground shake beneath me and the vibrations run up my legs as I jump down the stairs all the way to the lunch line where I'm finally safe, leaving behind a trail of fear.

~ • ~

My mom and I moved into my great-aunt's house in Granite Falls, Washington—about an hour away from my dad in Lynnwood—after my parents' separation. I hate everything about this year except for this house; it feels more like home than anywhere I've ever lived. My aunt and uncle make me feel welcome and heard. They encourage me in school, and I feel comfortable with myself around them.

After running away from my nightmare day at my new school, I sing along with Bob, their parrot, to try to escape thinking about what happened.

I can't even taste the snack mix I find in the pantry; I just want it in my mouth. When I've had my fill of that, I walk to the fridge and scavenge for something else to put in my stomach. I find a stir-fry packet, mushrooms, onions, and bell peppers, so I pull out a pan and cook all of it. When I finish that meal, I find an expired box of Girl Scout Tagalongs, open them, and shove them into my black hole. I end up eating half of them, then put the rest back. I go to my room, get under the covers, and try to sleep everything away.

~ • ~

After a week of enduring Melissa's dirty stares, sneers, and Instagram and Snapchat posts saying things like "I'm so tired of dealing with this fucking bitch," I finally decide to talk to an adult.

I pull the glass doors open that lead to the counseling office and find my counselor sitting at her desk. I take a seat in front of her. The skin on the back side of my thighs is cold, and goosebumps form on my legs.

I don't want to do this. Maybe I shouldn't.

"Why are you here?" she says, her nervous smile etched on her face, and something about the tone of her voice makes me sure she doesn't really want to hear why. I want to get up and walk out, but something makes me stay. As I start to recount what happened, I notice the deep lines of her crow's feet from constant smiling.

"What should I do?" I ask, after I explain and show her screenshots of the posts.

She gives me a dumbfounded look, but continues to smile.

"Well, I think you should play the invisible game." She pauses. "Don't let Melissa get to you. Pretend she's not there, even if she's yelling at you. Just pretend she's not there."

Invisible game? Cracks in my already fragile mind turn into chasms.

She's saying something about Melissa and how the death of her mother has affected her.

I feel nothing. I don't hear words anymore. I'm frozen. I try to process her words. She continues talking, and I hear a faint voice in my head protesting, telling me what she is saying is wrong.

I have no idea what it feels like to lose a parent, let alone be able to process it, but that doesn't give anyone the right to bully someone else.

I stare at her, get up, and go straight to the theater. I need to be surrounded by the safety of darkness.

~ • ~

Back at my aunt's house, I still feel as if I'm drifting away, floating above my body like a parade balloon.

I had the same feeling when my dad told me he had cheated on my mom. I could see the tops of our heads from above as we walked down the hill toward a convenience store. He said "I'm sorry, I'm sorry, I'm sorry, I'm sorry . . ." I kept floating far above until I couldn't see our heads anymore, just clouds and blue sky.

And I had the same feeling when I opened the door to my mom's room to find her crying and texting on her phone, looking defeated. Angry thoughts filled my head.

Why can't you get over it? Forget about him. I hate you and him both.

I'll never know why the adults in my life have never tried to help me, even when they knew I needed it. They all seem to turn a blind eye and pretend not to hear my cries for help, or see the blood dripping down my arms and stomach. Every time I'm treated like I'm invisible by an adult, a piece of me disappears. I feel like I have to glue everyone else back together as I crumble.

Can't anyone see that I'm hurting?

All of their empty words burn into my mind, like when a song gets stuck in your head and just won't leave.

Bob's singing lulls and I give in again. I eat so much that it hurts; the physical pain masks the emotional pain. I just want to eat anything that will make me forget. But when I look in the mirror, I remember that I want to cut away the fat.

~ • ~

The next day I go to the principal's office with my friend who knows the whole story. We show the principal the screenshots and I tell him everything. My friend tells him Melissa has bullied her, too.

"I'll do something about it if something comes up again," he says, without meeting my eyes.

I walk away knowing it's up to me to do something. I hear from everyone that Melissa's talking about me again. When lunch rolls around, I am filled with rage, searching for my prey. All I want to do is hit her.

I finally find her after pushing through the crowded lunch-room. I see her sitting outside, talking and laughing with some of the people I once called friends, blissfully unaware of the fire-ball heading her way. I march to the table where she sits and see the smile on her face disappear into a scowl. We lock eyes, and that's when the fire that is in my throat comes shooting out, burning her.

"Why am I still hearing my name in your mouth? Stop talking about me. Stop calling me a nigger."

Melissa narrows her eyes.

"I didn't say anything," she yells. "I never called you a nigger!"

"Stop lying!" My cheeks burn.

Disbelief fills her eyes.

"Why can't you just admit what you said?" I continue. "Get up! I'm so sick of your bullshit. Get up! I'm not going to tell you again."

"Shut up!" she yells, remaining seated. "Get out of here!" Her voice cracks.

"No!" I yell. "I wanna fight since you don't want to leave me alone."

I walk toward her, hunched over, spitting out the fire in my throat.

"Why can't you admit what you said? You're such a cunt!"

Her jaw drops and her eyes get big.

"What did you call me?" she asks as she gets up from where she's sitting to back away from me.

Really? That word is going to get to you? After calling me a nigger, you have the audacity to be bothered now?

"You heard me, bitch! Don't act like you didn't," I say.

I flex my arm and am ready to throw a punch when I feel someone grabbing my arm from behind.

"Go back inside," says a stern female voice. "This isn't the way to handle things."

I spin around to see yet another adult who just doesn't get it. I lock eyes with her and glare her down.

What is the way to handle things, then? Let the monster chew on my mind and gulp down my self-worth?

No way.

My heart is racing, and I can feel hundreds of eyes on me. I put my earbuds in to regain control and walk away to James Brown's song "I Got the Feeling."

"You don't know what you do to me / People are heavy, down in misery."

When I get to class, I tell the substitute I need to go see my counselor; I have to get out of here. I grab my backpack and rush out the door with the feeling of change all around me.

As I take my last step off of the stairs, I break into a run. I run as hard and as fast as my gorgeous, chunky legs will carry me, all the way home. I've got to be free of all the bullshit that has been said and done to me.

I've been trying to get validation from everyone else, but all I have is myself.

If I have to stand up for myself and be labeled that angry black woman to get people to listen, I'll do that. If I have to scare people by being myself, I'll do that. If I have to decide not to care about the pain anymore and just live, I'll do that.

I don't exactly know what I will do, but I will figure it out on my own.

Hey. Yeah. Alright.

for EVERYONE else

FROM THE AUTHOR

I am grateful for everything that happened, because these events changed me and made me evolve into someone who doesn't take shit from anyone. I am more confident in what I say and in who I am. I was heading down a bad path, hanging out with a crowd of negative people who didn't care about the future. When I started going to Scriber Lake, I found amazing friends and started on a positive path toward graduation. Now I hang out with good souls. We love being crazy and young together . . . we love to laugh. And we want to become more than just functioning adults in this society. We see beyond what is right here in front of us and want to have a purpose. We want our stories to open some people's eyes. We want to help others feel less alone and recognize they have a voice to change things for the better. The teachers at Scriber have also been very influential to me just by showing they cared. I want to be a librarian like Leighanne Law, Scriber's former librarian, because she recommended good books and always took time to listen. There is something about the Scriber community that is so effective— if you're willing to work at it. Being in quarantine these past months has made me see even more clearly that the problems I thought were world-ending are just little blips in time. People can call you whatever they want, but you are the only person who knows who you are. Words leave mental scars, but that doesn't mean they have to rule you. You get to decide what rules you and where your life is headed.

bit.ly/3hqiUiM

YOUTUBE CHANNEL
STEEP STAIRS PRESS

17

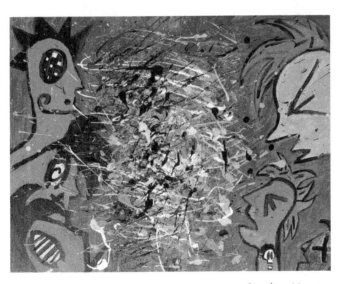

Speaking Monsters
Stephanie Souza
2019

ROOM 256

Dominic Severich

It feels like a dream how it all went. I had imagined it so many times that when it actually happened it didn't seem real. Not long ago she was crying in treatment because we were late to see her. Now, suddenly, she's moving into her own apartment—a halfway house—fifteen minutes north of us, in Everett, Washington.

It feels like she's made it, like she has all the resources she needs now to get where she wants to be in life, with a job and a support system in place. She can get back to being my mom.

I believe in her and hope she uses these opportunities to her advantage.

She looks drastically better than she has in a couple of years too; she's no longer a skeleton. Her nails are painted, and her skin is glowing. It seems like nothing can stop her from being happy in this moment. As I watch her unpack boxes of the things we had all been keeping for her—her owl knickknacks, candles, old prize silverware she found at the thrift shop—it's like watching a kid running through a ball pit with no worries in the world. She's feeling free, and her energy is contagious. I can't help but smile seeing her eyes filled with hope.

For a moment I forget all the bad that has happened since I was twelve years old, three years ago, and just focus on our recoveries: her recovery from heroin addiction and mine from the dark place I was in because of it.

~ • ~

As soon as my mom opened the door to her motel room, I felt a sense of home smelling her favorite candle: "Leaves" from Bath & Body Works. Her brown, wavy hair was pulled back into a classic red bandana. She hugged me tightly and I could feel the difference in her immediately.

"I love you," she said, tearing up. Her enthusiasm almost distracted me from the fact that she had lost almost forty-five pounds since the last time I saw her.

Is she okay? Is she sick? Why haven't I seen her in so long?

I asked myself these questions over and over again, as if asking was going to give me the answer I needed.

Just two days earlier, when I was in the car with my dad on I-5, he asked me a question out of nowhere: "Do you want to talk to your mom?"

"Sure," I said immediately and casually, but the question rushed through my body like a river through a canyon. It didn't make sense; it was the last thing I expected him to say.

My palms got all sweaty. *Where is she?* I wondered. I hadn't been told. All I knew was I hadn't seen her in months, and my mind spun with possible answers.

I waited for him to dial her number. He clicked in the numbers 2-5-6. *What the fuck is 256?* Those numbers didn't mean anything to me. I didn't like it.

Her voice shot out of the car speakers like a cannon and it hit me all at once.

"Hello, Baby Boy."

Emotions I didn't realize I had submerged like vessel wreckage in the middle of the ocean had just come to the surface. She asked me basic questions about sixth grade and football, then said, "Your dad's going to bring you to visit me this weekend. Hopefully. If you guys aren't busy."

I was confused. After months of not knowing where she was, I really didn't want to face the reality—whatever it was. *Reality can wait a little while longer*, I kept thinking as we drove.

But reality came quickly, and it was staring at me with hollow eyes and chipped nail polish.

My dad dropped me off in front of the Sea-Tac Motel 6, where she'd been living for the past couple of months. He told me to come out in forty-five minutes; he was uneasy with the whole thing. I could tell because he kept saying, "If you see anything that makes you uncomfortable, just come back out and we'll go somewhere else."

I found Room 256. *Now* the numbers meant something to me.

When my mom and I sat down I noticed one of her teeth was missing.

"What happened to your tooth?"

"Oh, I have to get a filling."

I just stared at her as she explained how her filling had fallen out, and that she planned to fix it. The mom I knew wouldn't have left her house with a tooth like that. *Why was this so much of my mom but so not?*

She got up and started to fix pillows, straightening the sheets as we talked. She asked me about school, sports, everything. I answered all of her questions, but I was afraid to ask her anything. She was acting so jittery that a feeling of dread overwhelmed me. My hands were sweaty and my stomach was in knots, but I kept it under control. For her. She is the single most important person in my life, and I wanted nothing other than to make her happy and to be happy with her.

I started to think about one of my favorite days with her as she talked. I was in the fourth grade, and it was a sunny, slightly breezy Friday afternoon. When I got off the bus, I found the back door open; the condo was airy and light music was coming out of the TV. The smell of spaghetti sauce hit me and transported me into a whole new dimension. It was like that scene in *Alice in Wonderland* when she finally steps out and sees that magical new world in front of her eyes. My mom was making my favorite dinner—Crock-Pot spaghetti and Texas toast. It was just the two of us. My sister was over at her friend's house and it was going to be "our day." She even went to the store and got us stuff to make strawberry shortcake. I loved days like this because she wasn't stressed out about anything. We would just sit on the back porch and let the sun take us out of our minds and into a deep, comfortable place while drinking lemonade or crunching on Otter Pops.

The sounds of construction took me out of my memories and back to Room 256—with the running toilet that was so obviously broken, the knockoff Vincent van Gogh paintings, and the owl knickknack things—where a clone of my mom was sitting right in front of me. The room felt like a bad dream dressed up as a good one. In it was everything I had and lost.

For months I had been staying up all night crying, missing her, wondering where she went, listening to her favorite song on repeat, until I heard birds chirping and saw the sun creeping up above the horizon. I took way too many sleeping pills to get out of the nightmare I was calling life, losing my peace of mind.

But I held onto this moment with her like a boa constrictor feasting on its first meal in weeks.

But her smile, god, her smile. It made me so happy, even though I know she was forcing it for me. She still smelled like sweet pea lotion and cigarettes. I looked at her funny and wondered if she could tell how I was reacting to this depressing version of what we had before.

Should I tell her how I feel? Will it ruin the moment? If I saw her sad, the whole day would feel wrong. The mom I used to know would try to get it out of me, but I didn't know this person. I had so much to process, my head started to whirl like a distorted kaleidoscope.

And just like that, our forty-five minutes was up.

She walked me through the hotel to get to the car. I saw a needle in the parking lot. I knew it was for drugs.

She greeted my dad. Then she hugged me and said, "I love you, Chanse." That was her nickname for me.

As we drove away, my dad asked, "How did it go?"

I answered with another question. "Why is she there?"

"She's made bad decisions."

~ • ~

For two years we waited for her to come to her senses, and we made multiple attempts to try to convince her to get clean. But we learned that the only way to get her clean was for her to want to get clean. The anxiety and stress started to take a toll on me. It affected every aspect of my life, from school to sports. I refused to go to family gatherings and felt random anger toward people. I had always been a pretty good student, so it was alarming to everyone when I started sleeping in class or just skipping it altogether. My dad tried his hardest to keep me stable, but he worked the night shift and I didn't see him a lot. I was going through it alone, waiting for the day that I would stop feeling bad for myself and get off my ass.

Finally, she admitted herself to rehab. After a month and a half, we were all waiting for my mom to come through the doors—my two aunts, my uncle, grandma, grandpa, brother, sister, and me. None of us would miss it for the world; we were the first ones there.

Of course she took longer than everyone else, and we knew it was because she wanted to look nice for us. We watched as other families met their loved ones, cried, hugged, and kissed. When she finally walked through the door, she looked like a whole new person. She looked healthy beyond comprehension—at least compared to what she looked like before. Most of us were crying; even I got a little teary seeing her. She came around and hugged all eight of us. But I got the first hug.

We sat at a table in a big room and talked for two hours. The rehab center was a lot less depressing than I thought it would be; it was somewhat colorful and welcoming. You could tell a lot of stories had gone through there and a lot of tears had been shed. I had to lighten the mood, so I was cracking jokes and making everyone feel a little less timid in this foreign territory. The workers were very open; some were past addicts. They explained how to ask questions without being too pushy.

I felt invincible. It was a day of progress, a day of forgiving and accepting—a perfect day. The breeze outside, the beaming sun shining on my aunt's jumbo-sized sunglasses on top of her head. We had been waiting for this day for years and it lived up to every expectation I had.

But that feeling didn't last long.

One month later my feet were in warm sand as I sat on a log and listened to the waves crashing outside of my aunt's beach house in Stanwood. The sky was purple, pink, and orange, and the sun was just about to sink. But I was sweating profusely, like I was taking the last shot in a championship game. When my brother called to tell me my mom had left the recovery house, it made me want to vomit everywhere. Suddenly my head was back to swimming in all the unknowns. *Where is she? Who is she with? How is she? Is she even alive?*

I had to get out and walk. My mind didn't tell me to; my body just did it.

Thinking of her sea glass collection, I picked up a piece to remind me of the days when heroin didn't ruin my life. It was comforting to feel the smoothness of the glass against my thumb and index finger as I thought about us being on the boat, coming back to the house, eating crab, and listening to country music. We used to stay up late by the campfire, and she and my aunt would make early morning coffee runs regardless of how much they had to drink the night before.

Why? She was doing so well. How could she let us go through all of this—let us help her move into rehab and everything—just to leave in the middle of the night without saying anything to anybody?

We all thought it was going to be okay, and then it just wasn't. Just like that.

When I went back inside, I looked at our old pictures as tears ran down my face. I knew that if she didn't take her blood pressure medicine for her bad heart, everything in the pictures would just become remnants of her past she would leave behind—along with me. Everyone else was out on the boat, so I laid down on the couch to watch *Madagascar* and escape back to childhood.

After a while, I could hear rain start to fall on the roof. It hadn't rained in a couple weeks; unusual for Washington. In the darkness, the sound of heavy rainfall pounding against the roof was my only comfort.

~ • ~

People are coming in and going out, helping us move furniture into her new apartment. Some come to the doorway to welcome her and offer support, people she knew from "the streets" who are also living there.

I'm waiting for all the chaos of the move to be over so we can have a real conversation. I feel a weird, timid awkwardness about it, though. The two of us hadn't talked about a lot of what had happened—her relapses, stealing money from friends and family, and her other reckless actions toward people who loved her—and how it all affected me. We only talked about these things during family meetings at rehab. I don't want there to be a chance to dodge questions or walk away from the conversation, so I'm waiting for the perfect timing. I feel if we can just clarify how we are feeling, we can get over it. Or at least accept it.

When everyone finally leaves and we sit down on the couch, she turns on the TV. I'm afraid I'm going to lose the moment. *It's now or never.* I have so many questions on my mind, but a starter question—nothing too much—just comes out of my mouth.

"How are you feeling about everything?" I ask.

She turns to me with a tentative, worried face. It looks like she is scared but ready for change. She's willing to discuss things with me.

"I feel great," she answers. She goes on to tell me about all the stuff she wants to do, where she wants to put things, how she wants to build some closets.

It seems like a genuine answer, not an act. "I'm excited for you," I say. "Everything is great, you deserve it." I have to add my usual sarcasm, though. "You'd better not mess it up!"

She laughs nervously, and gives me her "I know you" look.

I decide to leave the small talk and come out with the question that has really been on my mind.

"What did it for you? Did someone do something to push you over the edge? What was the last straw that made you finally break?" I feel tense asking her these things, and realize I am fiddling with a loose strand on the couch. But I really want to know. I haven't ever struggled with the disease of addiction or how it feels to be the reason you lose your family. The person I knew before would never have done what she did; I knew it must have built up over time.

She pauses, surprised at the question. But she answers honestly. She describes the emotional turmoil in her life and how it affected all of the decisions she made. Her boyfriend at the time was doing pills, and she started doing them with him as a way to relax from the stress of getting laid off from her work.

"When we got evicted, that's where it got worse," she says.

We had to stay with my aunt, and my mom started relying more on pills. Not long after the eviction, she sold her car, moved into the Motel 6, and started doing heroin.

She was nervous talking about it. I could tell by the way she fidgeted and moved around. That made me feel good, because I knew she wasn't faking it.

When her tone started to sound defensive, I wanted to put her at ease.

"I will never hold anything against you," I said. "I will always be there for you no matter what. I do have bad days, but I will do my best not to take it out on you."

Her whole body relaxes. It's like a thorn has been taken out of her back and she is finally feeling some relief. She's trying not to cry.

I don't want to show her the side effects of what she has done to me. I want her to be able to be full-on progressing without worrying about me. I don't want to come off as a threat. This conversation isn't like the others that we had as a family; this is an actual conversation, not an interrogation.

She is no longer struggling to answer anything, and that gives me a great deal of comfort. Little does she know I have been over this conversation hundreds of times in my head. I want it to go just right and set the tone for all future conversations. I am not emotionally ready for anything to set her back at all. She has to be resilient and have thick skin.

"I'm sorry, Chanse. I never meant to hurt you."

I cut her off to reassure her that I'm not mad at her, and that I don't want an apology. I need her to know that even if she isn't her full self now, I will be there until she is. And after that, too. That I need her just as much as she needs me.

"I've done research. I know it's a disease," I say. "You had no intention to do this. It wasn't you. You were severely addicted, and that altered your mind and your decision-making."

"Thank you," she says. "But I'll be better. You're my ride or die, you know."

"I know."

We have always looked out for each other, and have always been able to talk transparently. We never had secrets until the heroin.

This honesty has to go beyond the two of us, though. Some people in my family aren't expressing their pain, and I know that we have a long way to go, that recovery will be a lifetime thing. I want to be clear that this is the first step. Anything can happen.

"You can't let your pride get in the way," I tell her. "You're not the trustworthy person you used to be. Don't take it personally. Just take it day by day, and everyone will come around."

"I love you," she says, and we hug.

I feel an understanding pass between us about all of the progress that has taken place in just a few weeks. We can turn our attention back to the TV and have a normal time now. I said what I wanted to say, and it went like I wanted it to.

I had no idea at the time, but that conversation was an important step on my own road to recovery as well. I went from being a negative person who didn't have a vision for his future to the exact opposite. Why not be upbeat and happy? Why not make someone laugh when they don't feel like it? Why not have a good attitude? I had to teach myself to do this on a consistent basis. I had to teach myself to appreciate life.

~ • ~

Almost one year after that conversation, as I walked up the wet stone steps of Scriber Lake High School, I felt nothing but relief realizing that it was the start of something new, of something I had been yearning for: a clean slate. I was nervous, but the familiar smell of the trees and the comfort of the friendly faces coming down the stairs took me out of my own head. I knew I was ready and responsible for my own future.

FROM THE AUTHOR

My mom has been clean for two years now and is in the process of moving to an apartment next to my brother and sister, which is also a lot closer to me. During quarantine, she and I have had time to talk about everything, and we agree that we've reached a place where we are more at peace with our experiences than we are sad about them. It's been good to be able to clarify everything together and feel happy about where we are. I decided to write this story because I needed validation for my own feelings; writing this makes it seem like the hard times I went through were not for nothing. I can relate to August Alsina's song "Cry" when he sings "They say a man ain't supposed to cry / so I'mma let the song cry." I've been able to express a lot by writing this, and I hope that anyone who reads it will know that whatever they are going through is completely okay and that they are not alone. I know that is what everyone says, but it really is true. I want everyone to feel validated in their feelings instead of hiding away like I did. When I got to Scriber, I saw a new light and started to take advantage of my opportunities; before then, I wasn't really living life. I was just going through it. And now that I am doing better in school, I can figure out my future goals with a clear head. In the same way that my mom is the only one who can decide to stay clean, I am the only one who can decide what I'm going to make of my own life. Now I want to be someone's light in their darkness; helping someone else get through theirs helps me get through mine. I want to be held accountable for being a good, decent person. I want everything I do to be done with purpose.

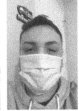

YOUTUBE CHANNEL
STEEP STAIRS PRESS

bitly/3hqiUiM

31

Fear
Stephanie Souza
2019

HOW TO BE A MIME

Stephanie Souza
aka Rainbow Disco Queen

Jackie, Seraiah, and I are sitting in the back of the blue school van, headbanging to our favorite songs. Dominic and Emil are on their phones in the middle seat. And Marjie, our teacher, is driving. Marjie just explained that we are on our way to speak at a Lifespan Psychology class at Edmonds Community College. The class is studying the teenage years right now, and the students want to hear our stories.

I get really nervous every time we go somewhere to read, but I try really hard not to show it. Usually I mess up some of the words when I begin because I'm worrying about how people might react. We want our stories to be heard because we give them our everything. We relive our past pain and struggles in front of our audiences. For most of us, it's hard to keep going back to the places we write about.

At the reading just before this one, a few older men in the audience were talking during Jackie's story, and we saw a lot of people on their phones. That made us all feel uncomfortable—like they were disrespecting our stories, our lives.

I hope it's not like that today.

This is what's on my mind all the way to the college, but a couple things make me feel comfortable as soon as we enter the classroom. For one, there are only about fifteen people in the room. And for another, a guy with tattoos all over his muscular arms sits at a table in the front wearing a white lace dress. *How cool.*

Not many guys would do that with confidence, which is not cool. People should express themselves any way they want.

While everyone gets settled, I display my art cards on a table near the back window with a sign that says "Cards $3 each." For the past year I've been making prints of my paintings and creating cards out of them to sell at readings like this. Everywhere I go at least a couple of people will buy a card and say how much they like my art. Right now I have several copies of about fifteen different paintings. When I finish placing them on the table, I join everyone else in a row of seats in front.

Seraiah reads first, then Jackie. I can tell this audience is interested because they are taking notes and asking questions after each story. I don't notice anyone on a phone, and no one is talking. I feel respected.

They all seem comfortable with their own weirdness. Before one guy asks a question, he introduces himself as "Thunder." He explains his mom named him that because he was born during a storm.

That sounds like the beginning of a superhero movie. I want my name to be something as cool as that.

After all five of us finish reading, the guy in the white lace dress stands up and looks at me.

"I love your art," he says. "I want everyone to have a card. Here's $60. I think that's enough for everyone in the room to choose one."

I'm in shock. It's always shocking to me when someone buys even one card, but twenty . . . it doesn't seem real.

"I want all of you to have one, too," he says to my friends. "And your teacher."

Everyone walks to the table to choose a card, and it's really cool to hear their reactions. I hear them saying things like "This one has so much emotion in it" or "I love how the bright colors contrast with the sad characters." I want to ask every one of them why they chose their card.

"What do you think about when you're making this art?" Thunder asks me after choosing the one with the sad flower.

"It's hard to explain. My brain is so chaotic, my characters come to me out of nowhere. I might start out with a squiggle, then start adding faces that represent a feeling I have."

He tells me his girlfriend does art, but that she can only do it when she's going through depression. "Do you need to be depressed to do this?"

"Not really. It just depends on what I'm feeling at the moment I'm making it."

I like it when people ask me questions like these. After years of being made to feel like I was stupid and worthless, I finally feel like I mean something. Like I am no longer a ghost. For years, I walked through my days feeling like no one could see or hear me.

~ • ~

When I get home after the reading, I sit on the couch for a minute, just thinking about everything. I can't believe that one year ago I was in such a bad emotional place. But I survived, I'm here, and now people are connecting with my art. *My art is helping people to see something inside themselves they haven't seen before.*

For a few years I completely stopped showing my art to people; I decided to just keep it to myself when some of my friends laughed at it. *All I can probably do with my life is sell ice cream, or maybe be a bus driver,* I would tell myself. Now people want to buy my art, and they always ask where I get my ideas for paintings. That's a hard question, because I think about a lot of things as I paint—usually random things I see during the day, like a person sitting by themselves just texting or wearing a cool hat.

One time I saw someone on the bus wearing the coolest clown makeup, and I gave them flowers because I had some with me and I loved how they expressed themselves.

"Are these for me? Thank you!" they said.

"Yes! I love your makeup."

They smiled really big, and it made me so happy to make someone else happy.

I can look at someone like that and say, "They are an art piece. They aren't doing anything, but they are an art piece." The guy in the white lace dress was definitely an art piece.

Or I might even see art when I look at a piece of paper sitting on the ground.

People always mention how "dark" my art is, which is something I can't control. All of my paintings capture whatever emotion I'm feeling at the time. I think I have crackhead energy. A lot of people at Scriber ask me if I do drugs—like acid—when I make art. They are in shock when I say no.

One time my sister wanted me to paint something "happy," so I tried to paint a happy bunny. She thought it was cute but looked crazy and depressed. That's just the way it comes out of me.

I ponder Thunder's question. What do I think about while I'm painting? I'm extremely expressive, for one thing. When my family is out of the house, I will put headphones on and either headbang to my favorite songs or listen to quiet piano music. I might be sobbing, or I might be extremely happy. Sometimes I don't know how I feel. I could be really zoned out and quiet, or I could be yelling out random stuff. Most of my paintings flash me back to the past. When I look at one of them I can remember exactly what was happening the day I made it. Sometimes, though, I think about my friends, or about my future and how that will look.

That's what I'm thinking about right now.

All of this happened in just one day. What's going to happen next year? And the year after that?

Dude, I feel ok.

FROM THE AUTHOR

I have known for a long time—way before high school—that I wanted to write my story. Being placed in the wrong special ed class since the third grade and having no voice to get out of that situation was really hard, so I used to write notes on my old phone to get it out. When I went to the book release for Scriber's 2019 book, *Listen*, and heard other students read their stories, I knew I wanted to write and publish my story, too. I wanted my story to help others like hearing those stories helped me.

I spent the next two years writing. I was eager to get everything out, but it was really difficult because many scenes were hard to relive. Many times I had to get up and walk out of the room to get myself together. I started to read parts of my story in front of groups of people right before everything shut down for COVID-19. Sharing it was really cool because I got to see people's reactions and experience how they genuinely cared. It was so nice. Writing helped heal me.

Everything was going really well until everything shut down. I began to really struggle with my mental health because of what was going on in the world. I was filled with anxiety seeing protests and teargas. The world was on fire and I could do nothing to help. I just didn't want to leave my house. Sometimes I would make a goal to take the trash out, but in the end it was just too hard even to do that. I wasn't on medicine that would help me with my anxiety then, so it was really bad. I didn't want to join Zooms at all. If anyone asked if I needed help, I would just say no, even though I did. I wanted to drop out.

I also started thinking way too much about how people would respond to all the details of my story. I realized that publishing my whole story wasn't something I was ready for. I decided to put a part of it (titled "How to Be a Mime") in this year's book for a couple reasons, including that it details the first time a stranger bought my art. I hope to publish the rest of it when I know I am 100% ready. I also hope to someday make books about mental health issues for little kids.

Behind every title, there's a story. I saw my special ed class like a freak show. All of us were performers, trying to make people laugh and amaze them with our abilities. All the other students were the audience throwing trash at us, yelling "Boo!" The teachers were like conductors, trying to turn us into mimes without a voice. But we didn't want to be mimes. We all wanted to be heard, to be free. We wanted to bring joy to people when they saw us, not fear or disgust.

Finally, having my art on and in this book means so much to me. I never thought that would happen because people always made fun of it when I was growing up. My story is represented in these paintings, so I hope they help people heal. I hope people feel seen and understood when they look at them; that's my hope for me, too.

bit.ly/3hqiUiM

YOUTUBE CHANNEL
STEEP STAIRS PRESS

for EVERYONE else

Anti-Depressants
Stephanie Souza
2019

NOW I BREATHE

Kayla Claggett

I stare at the ground as I walk up the driveway, keeping in the tears. My uncle and his friends are standing around the barbecue, and I hope they can't tell something is up. My mom's best friend—the one I talk to when I have problems with my mom— is the only other person outside. She holds a cigarette and is staring at me with questioning eyes.

"I tried to say no . . ." I manage, finally letting the tears fall.

She shakes her head and says, "Go talk to your mom." At times she knows she can't be the person in the middle, but her response seems harsh. My stomach twists at the thought of seeing my mom.

As I enter the house, I expect mom to gut me for not coming straight home from school. She is standing next to my grandparents by the stove, her long brown hair in a bun.

"I tried to tell him no," I say, and more tears escape.

Her eyes fill with horror as her mind registers what has happened.

"He hurt my baby!" she screams. Then she runs outside and screams again, "He hurt my baby!"

She yells it over and over. I stand there, frozen, as she keeps running in and out of the house screaming. Now everyone outside knows everything. The last thing I want.

"Who?" my uncle says as he appears in the kitchen. His face is straight and tense.

"Calvin," I tell him.

He walks back outside and yells, "Get in the fucking car!" to his friends. Then I hear the engine speeding down the street. My uncle is more like my brother; we grew up together, and he is a sophomore, only a year older. And he is a big guy, so I know if he finds Calvin it will not end well. He is extremely overprotective when it comes to his family.

What is he going to do? Does he know where Calvin lives?

Even though they go to the same school, they don't talk. They aren't friends. Calvin and I, however, we used to be kind of friends. We were in the same drama class, but I had stopped going. We hung out during lunch a few times. We talked a bit on Snapchat.

But not after today. Never again after today. I know nothing will ever be the same.

~ • ~

I try to piece the day together.

Calvin texted me earlier asking if I wanted to skip with him. I felt uneasy about it, so I told him no. I had been skipping Drama ever since the second week of school, when the teacher humiliated me in front of everyone.

I told the counselor I didn't want to be in Drama anymore, that I'd rather be in any other class. But she said all of the other classes were full, so I found a simple solution to my problem: I didn't go. The teacher didn't understand how easy it was to mess up with a whole class judging you, how easy it was for the lines to slip your mind. He didn't know I was trying to text my mom because of the anxiety attack I was about to have when my teacher started yelling at me. At that moment, everyone knew I wasn't going to come back to that class again. And I didn't.

I usually go with Sally to the south woods—where kids go to smoke—but all Sally ever does is talk behind my back. She and Sydney talk about how I'm such a slut, how I'm a ho, how I'm an attention seeker. They fill my life with toxicity and drama. Most of the time I don't know why I'm even friends with them.

My phone rang right after we got to the Burger King behind the school, and I knew who it was before I looked at the screen.

"Where the hell are you?" my mom asked.

"I'm at school. What do you mean?" I said. I knew she knew I wasn't, but if I told her the truth she'd only yell at me more.

"I know you aren't. Get your ass back to school," she said, then continued with her normal lecture about the Becca Bill and how she wasn't going to get in trouble for me not going to school. She was at work so she could only lecture me for so long. She hung up.

I knew she was going to be pissed, but when was she not mad at me? I never go to class anymore, so this is nothing new. The only class I like is science. My science teacher is my favorite because I can talk to her. She seems to know I'm struggling, so she tries to make things easy for me. But me skipping and making my mom unhappy—this is becoming a regular conversation.

I went back to school just to go to science. After school, I saw Calvin out front.

"Want to come over for a while?" he asked, his blue eyes piercing into mine. I was hesitant, but he persisted. He grabbed my backpack and pulled me toward him. *Whatever*, I thought, and I started walking with him. My mom always worked until six, and I told my grandparents I was going to a homework club after school. No one knew where I was.

I keep thinking about how one decision changed everything. *What if I had just decided not to go? What if I didn't hang out with those people? None of this would be happening now . . .*

~ • ~

I grab my dog Muffin, sit on the couch, and stare straight ahead. Everyone around me is freaking out, too loudly. I just need time to take a moment. I need time to freeze, just for a second.

Is any of this real?

My grandma is on the phone with the police, pacing the living room and kitchen.

Please just be a nightmare.

My mom is all over the place. Tears still stream down my

face, and my throat feels like it is closing. I am suffocating in my thoughts. My only source of comfort is my dog, who lies innocently in my lap. I try to focus on petting her soft white fur, just trying to forget. Forget about my family flipping out. Forget about everything that happened not even an hour ago. Can't we just forget about it?

Maybe life is just a cruel joke. A sick, cruel, twisted joke. Where is the good? I haven't seen it in years. Maybe it's all me. Maybe I just don't deserve anything good out of life. Maybe it's all my fault. I said no multiple times. He didn't stop.

I should have done more. I shouldn't have caved. I said no, though. What did he not get about no? I said no so many times.

My mom will want a court case to go forward. He is only sixteen. He told me once about wanting to be a filmmaker. What if I take his dreams away from him? At the same time, what if he did it to himself? What if he did to others what he did to me?

"She's not going back to that damn school!" my mom yells to my dad over the phone, throwing off my thought process. My dad lives four hours away—why is she calling him?

The moment one traumatic thing happened during his sobriety, she went to him. Even though she knew how unstable he could be, she told him all about what went wrong with her other ex-husband. *Why does he get to know everything? He couldn't even bother to get clean until he was forced to go to rehab many times. Why does he get to know what happened when he can never get his act straight? Why does he get to know when he couldn't bother to be in his daughters' lives?*

My mom had stayed with him for six years, for my sake.

Recently he had been back in my life to a point; before this, sixth grade was the last time I saw him. He showed up at school on my birthday that year. He gave me a balloon and a card.

After that I texted him a few times, wanting to know when I'd see him again. But I knew that he was getting to a very low point. Just a few weeks before, when his girlfriend at the time was driving me home from a weekend at his house, he was chugging a bottle.

"What are you doing?" I asked, because I knew he had a problem.

"Stress drinking," he replied.

Of course.

After that birthday, those few minutes were the last time I saw him for three years. Alcohol has been his problem for a while. Even if he was sober and working on it, we knew it wouldn't last long. He was a terrible person when he drank. We hadn't needed him for years, so why did we need him now? Lord only knows what he had been doing. I didn't want to know.

My racing thoughts are quickly shut down when the ambulance and police arrive. Suddenly I find myself in a series of different rooms. With a series of people. A series of the same questions. A white room, with a hospital bed, chairs along the wall next to the bed. A small room with a round table and chairs around it, a camera in the corner. A waiting room. A little bland room. A man with balding gray hair. A small woman with glasses and short curly hair. A woman with long brown hair. Anxiety eats away at me. Everything is a blur.

Many people come in and out of the white room. Multiple nurses shove pills down my throat. One injects a needle into my thigh. The first person to walk in who isn't medically focused is the man with CPS, the man with balding gray hair. He has a flyer about sexual assault and explains exactly what happened to me to make sure I understand. He asks questions. He asks many questions. The questions make it feel real. I don't want it to feel real. I wish it wasn't real. Maybe any minute I will wake up from this nightmare.

"Did you feel threatened?"

"Did he force you to do anything orally?"

He asks detailed questions that eat at me. I feel uncomfortable, weak. I just want to go home. The amount of time he talks feels like an eternity. It's never ending. I just want it to end. I want to go home. I want to sleep.

After he leaves it's more nurses, then the police. Most of the questions are the same. Is this just going to be a series of answering the same questions?

The nurse with brown hair that had blonde highlights, however, is my favorite. She happens to be the woman who did the cotton swabs to try and get any DNA that was left. She also took pictures of any marks that were left on my body. I feel gross. I just need a long shower. Both she and the paramedic in the ambulance got my mind off of what happened by talking about everything except what happened, like my interest in art. Nothing felt real, my body didn't feel like my own, but they both helped to put me at ease and get my mind off the trauma I was left to face. All I wanted throughout that time, though, was just to go home. Lie in my own bed. Be with my dog.

~ • ~

After five hours we are still in the hospital. It's late, completely dark. A knock on the door, then a tall, buff man enters. My dad. He must have driven all the way to the hospital as soon as he got the call from my mom. I didn't want him to know. The only people I even see on that side of my family are my grandpa and his wife. They're the only ones I get along with.

"Hey, baby. How are you?" he says in his deep voice. He looks remorseful. He's always had sad eyes and a small smile that looks fake, but it's different when something is actually bugging him. I can tell he is hurting.

Either way, he has come to drive us home. He makes a pit-stop for me on the freeway because all the pills they put into my system make me feel nauseous.

~ • ~

Another day. A small room with a camera in it. The room fills me with anxiety. *What if the detective doesn't even believe me?* She is a short lady with glasses and curly hair. Expressionless. She scares me most out of all the people I have talked to. Whatever happens next depends on whether she believes me or not. She asks so many questions, detailed questions. I have to give detailed answers. I feel uncomfortable, and my reaction when I feel uncomfortable, of course, is to laugh. *What if she doesn't be-*

lieve me? I don't even want to be going through this process, but my family wants me to press charges. What if I am just messing everything up?

"Were there drugs involved?"

"Did he penetrate vaginally?"

The questions make me feel sick, weak. They make me feel like nothing. *She doesn't believe me. She thinks I'm lying.*

In the end, though, she says the same thing my family keeps saying: "It will stop him from doing this to someone else."

That may be true. But the thought of going to court, the possibility of seeing him and having to say what happened in front of him, the chance that everything will get turned back on me. This is what scares me the most.

I can't even say his name without getting a panic attack. I just want to go home, curl up in a ball, and hide. I don't know what she's thinking. I sure as hell can't read her. She just takes notes, even though a camera records everything.

More questions. I recognize most of them—I've already had to fill out many questionnaires about my depression and anxiety, but now I'm answering questions about PTSD, about a specific event.

Next thing I know I am in a little bland room. A lady with long brown hair greets me. I am pretty sure she is a psychiatrist. She seems gentle and nice. I bet she sees so many people with so many different stories, and she hears it all. She sees how damaged some people are before events cause them even more pain. I'm guessing she can't make judgments, though, which is probably why the first thing she says after reading my assessment from the questionnaire is, "Wow, this shows that your depression, anxiety, and PTSD are severe." Severe. One word: very great, intense. An intense amount of depression, anxiety, post-traumatic stress disorder.

I don't care though. It feels like something I have to live with. In sixth grade, I just thought I was sad, but throughout my first year of middle school my mental state declined quickly. I never recognized my anxiety until I was diagnosed with it.

At that time, the only meal I would eat was dinner, and I only ate then because my mom forced me to. Insomnia and depression were my best friends. I filled the void with a blade on my skin most nights, and one night I filled it with painkillers. I didn't realize that doing so would only make me feel like shit the next day. I left school early because I was puking, and my family just thought I was sick. The friends that I did have were terrible. They tore me apart.

I haven't been able to imagine a month ahead in my life for so long. I genuinely think I will be dead by the time I am supposed to graduate. My head is constantly filled with demons eating away at any happiness I have left. This feels like something that will never go away.

"Has your family talked to you about therapy?" the psychiatrist asks.

"My mom is looking into it," I tell her, but therapy seems like a trap to eat up all of my mom's money. As though we're stacked on cash. As though she doesn't have a family to feed and take care of. As though bills aren't a thing. Besides, what's the whole point in therapy? I feel awkward. What am I supposed to talk about? What am I supposed to say? The whole idea feels weird. It may work for others, but I think therapy may just not be my thing. I don't know, maybe I'm just weird.

In the car, I am numb. I'm finally going home, but I wonder if I will ever not feel tired again. "I love you, Kayla," my mom says. "Everything is going to be okay." I want to believe her.

Depression. Loneliness. Insomnia. They all feel like things that will stick with me forever. Happiness just doesn't seem like a possibility for me. Maybe I don't deserve it. Maybe I deserve all the pain.

FROM THE AUTHOR

Happy. One word. Meaning: feeling or showing pleasure or contentment. Something I once thought I'd never be. Something I once thought was a myth. And yet, rolling down this street, with the sound of the skateboard wheels on the pavement, I feel more at peace in my chaotic life than I have in a while.

I have a family that sticks by me, even when I fall. And I have real friends who genuinely want to help me get further in life than I ever imagined.

Switching schools got all the negativity out of my life. Now I don't know how I was able to self-harm, and I don't want to be back in bed curling up all day.

Now I'm scared of dying because I've finally started living. Now I breathe because I want to, not because I need to. Now I get up in the morning ready to take on the day.

YOUTUBE CHANNEL
STEEP STAIRS PRESS

bit.ly/3hqiUiM

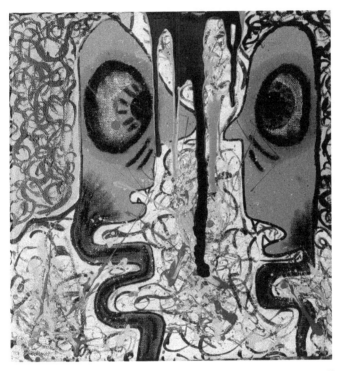

Look at Yourself
Stephanie Souza
2020

GHOSTING

Emil McDonald

On my way to my former hideout, I fumble over the broken concrete, the tree roots winning against the man-made path. When I get to the bent, green-stained chain link fence, I peer down the slope of the hill into the wooded area below. I used to want to jump down there, just to see what would happen.

These surroundings force me to relive a memory, turning present winter into near-summer past. I turn and see a younger Emil huddled up in a spot cleared of pine needles against the brick building. The upper wall is painted a darker color to hide graffiti that might as well say my ghost's name, as if it is a tombstone. He is on the verge of tears as I walk up to him, stand inside this imprint of myself, and sit down to relive the worst point in my life.

Dealing with my past trauma has been a journey, and I'm at the place where I can face it head-on.

~ • ~

It was almost summer break and my life was falling apart. The ants and spiders on the ground looked so calm compared with the thoughts swirling in my head. *Just focus on your work*, I told myself. *Martin Luther King Jr., botany, more history.* But frustration seized my chest and I grabbed my face to calm down. *I can't be near anyone right now.* No one else knew what had happened the night before, and I didn't want to make it a huge thing by telling everyone. But keeping it in was almost suffocating me.

It isn't even a big deal, I kept telling myself. I had been trying to believe this all throughout our relationship.

The chirping of the birds seemed foreboding as voices battled in my head.

Tyler must be so mad at me, said one voice.

Shut up, snapped another.

Our homeschool schedule included free periods where we could either hang out in the parent/teacher room, in the courtyard, or on the playground. Usually, I would be with a group of about ten friends, which included Tyler. But I had found a place to hide behind the school, and I could remain invisible at least through the end of the period and lunch. After that, I knew, I would have to return to classes.

He's going to make me feel the same way he always does, I thought. I would be afraid of him, and then I would go back to loving him. I would cry over something he said to me, always something that seemed small and insignificant, but his tone and his anger would leave me with a vaguely unsettled feeling. Then I would rationalize it all and go back to idolizing him. It had been our pattern for a year and a half.

Tyler and I met outside of our seventh-grade math class. I noticed his long, curly, burgundy hair. He noticed my My Chemical Romance hairbow.

"I like your bow," he said.

"Thank you," I answered, and we kept talking until the teacher came. I started liking him and soon we started "dating"—and by that I mean we had mutual crushes on each other. He wasn't allowed to date anyone until he was sixteen, which was two years away. I was okay with waiting, though. I had been in a deep depression because of my grandma's death, and the depression just never stopped. Of course, he had issues with depression and anxiety as well, so I felt like I had someone who understood me. It seemed like a pretty safe way to have a relationship: see each other at school and text from home. But it had turned into something toxic.

~ • ~

The night before, I had seen on Snapchat that Madeline, one of my friends, was smoking pot with thirteen- and fourteen-year-olds—kids who were three years younger than she. Madeline was letting people ride around in her car with the seats down and letting them roll around on top of them. I freaked out. Tyler knew her better, so I texted him about it. He texted me back:

> is this abt a thing you actually saw or...?
>
> yeah
>
> can we not talk about this please
>
> im sorry
>
> its okay you have a right to be worried i just dont wanna talk about this
>
> i know im sorry
>
> maybe possibly vent to someone else

I felt completely brushed off.

I sobbed. I went through a ton of tissues, even though I had no idea why I was crying so much. *Am I making a big deal about nothing?* The crying episodes kept getting worse and worse every time something like this happened. Each thing felt so minor, but my reactions said otherwise. I never told anyone, because I thought no one would care. Why would they when I shouldn't have cared either?

Guilt shadowed over me. None of the others had done anything, but even so, I started avoiding my other friends. The fight was all I could think about, and I didn't want to drag anyone into it. But if it wasn't a big deal, why couldn't I just tell someone?

What if they find me out here? I really don't want to talk to anyone or cause any drama. Why am I so terrified about that conversation?

When the bell rang, I ninja'd myself to the cafeteria so I could grab lunch and come straight back to my safe haven—I just wanted it to be me and the wall and the trees again. I felt so tired. I was about to spiral back into guilt when I heard voices on the other side of the wall. My breath caught in my throat. *Oh my god, did they follow me here?*

I flinched when two of my friends separated from the others and came into view. They were laughing, having a good time. I could see them, but they couldn't see me. Like I was a ghost.

I have to deal with this for a whole hour?

They pretended like they were going to jump the fence, but they eventually sat down to eat with the others. I could hear words coming from the group, but nothing registered through my panic. I was stuck floating in a cocktail of emotions: frustration, panic, guilt, dread. A caged animal.

God, I don't want to go to class.

The clock kept ticking, too slow and too fast all at once. I could still hear them. *What if he's with them? I don't want to see him. Why can't everyone just leave?*

The sickness and terror were peaking, and I was trying hard not to cry again. Their voices still filled my right ear, and they were starting to sound grating, like they were sawing at my skull.

When the lunch bell rang I took a deep breath, grabbed my things, and walked as quickly as I could past them. Suddenly their voices went silent. I could feel them looking at me.

Stop, please let me go. Just let me go.

"Whoa, I didn't know you were there," one of them said, a bit concerned.

I just shrugged.

Another chimed in, "Are you okay?"

I laughed halfheartedly. "Yeah, I'm okay, just . . . Yeah." I shrugged again, and walked away quickly.

He wasn't even with them.

A few nights later, he called me a bunch as I was watching the movie *Hidden Figures* with my mom and aunt, so I texted him.

> i still wanna talk about this...but you don't...so im kind of stuck here...and dont know what to do.

what?

...the stuff from saturday

what happened saturday
again?

My whole body tensed. I was confused. There is no way he didn't remember; he had even tried to talk to Madeline about it. I reminded him.

i can't control what she does
emma

My body felt heavy and light and like absolutely nothing all at once. Like static.

It was the first time he had called me by my dead name. He should've known how that would affect me because he is trans, too. Even if my mom still didn't know my name, he always called me by the name I had given myself, Emil. And I wasn't asking him to control Madeline. He was closer with her, so I thought he could talk to her and get her to see the danger in what she was doing. He started getting angrier, trying to convince me I was in the wrong.

you can't control what i do and
honestly i just don't care anymore
about anything

He didn't understand what I was saying. He didn't understand me at all. I gave up, threw my phone down on my mom's bed, and laid my head in her lap as I cried. She knew Tyler and I were having problems, but neither of us knew how significant they were. I let her look at what he said to me.

"You need to decide if this is how you want to be treated or not," she said.

He kept texting me. He wouldn't stop.

He won't listen to me. Has he always been like this? I don't know if I can do this. I don't want to do this.

I tried to pay attention to the movie, but my world seemed to be crashing around me. I wanted to be in a mutually supportive relationship. I wanted him to listen to me as much as I was willing to listen to him. The choice of whether or not I should leave was putting me into a suicidal state I hadn't been in for months. This just kept happening. He was always misunderstanding, and I was constantly trying to explain things. He'd been dismissive and angry for almost a week now, and it felt like it was never going to end. I didn't think it was fair, and I was questioning what was "normal."

The first time I can remember this happening was about a year before, after we had been in a relationship for several months. By that time, most of our tense interactions were over text. I was afraid to communicate with him face-to-face because of his extreme reactions.

At that time, he was struggling with his appearance. I couldn't understand how he thought he was ugly. I texted him with all my heart.

> if it's anything i think youre beautiful

> listen im not in the mood for lies right now

I froze. A strange anxiety welled up in my chest and my throat. It was as if he'd slapped me in the face. He was upset, I knew he was upset, but he was lashing out at me for trying to help him.

I pressed on. He had to know I was telling the truth. I texted through the fear-driven tears that were starting to come up.

> im not lying

> whatever

Then the tears came.

God, I think he hates me. Why is he so angry? Did I say something wrong?

From there, his behavior continued, and we fought more frequently. It seemed like every communication required me to walk on eggshells. Every time I was happy, he would shoot me down.

On the last day of school, he walked up to me during field day as I was sitting around with some friends. He pressured me to sign his yearbook. Later in the day, he texted me when I was with a group of friends lying around on the grass at a party.

> are you going to ignore me
> for the entire summer?

He started to rant about how none of it was his or Madeline's fault, how I was in the wrong. It was basically a long text that amounted to "sorry that you're upset."

My hand tightened around my phone in anger.

He kept confusing me. One minute he expected me to care, and the next I wasn't even allowed an opinion.

I tried to explain things, once again.

> i care. thats what i do...this is
> actual danger...illegal shit...and
> you know what?? i cant talk to
> you if you wont actually listen
> to me and understand what im
> saying. i cant. do this.

> im gonna go.

> how could you think that? who
> do you think i am? fine. whatever,
> have fun.

My mood was ruined and I didn't want to talk to anyone. I left the party early.

Two days later, I went to the musical theater awards ceremony night as a plus one to support my friend who was getting an award. Tyler texted me again, but I ignored it and watched everyone on stage. I had to take my binder off after the ceremony because I had left it on for too long. I was feeling lightheaded and was holding onto others to keep from falling.

A friend walked up to me and surprised me by saying, "You and Madeline need to talk." I had no idea my friend knew anything about it. She dragged me away from everyone and brought me to Madeline, who was standing with one of her friends. Madeline's light blue eyes seemed to shine with pride.

"I heard you have a problem with me," she said, smiling with self-righteousness. "You do know that what I'm doing isn't actually *wrong*, right?"

She and her friends started to laugh.

"Sorry, we're not laughing at you," she said. "It's just that you're the only one who cares about this."

My face burned with embarrassment, but it quickly turned into anger. Tyler was the only one I had told. The thought that he would betray me made my heart feel like it was being ripped out of my chest. I willed my light-headed body to move away from them. The person I came to support was gone. I stood and waited for him by a skinny tree in the courtyard as I desperately tried to make sense of everything. But nothing felt right anymore. My world felt broken.

I found out through friends that Tyler told Madeline I had a beef with her instead of telling her the truth, which was that I was worried about her safety. I had had enough. I broke up with him. I felt nothing for a while after that. I'd already cried enough. The littlest things helped me cope, like drawing on myself, or eating Lucky Charms because he hated them. I ripped up every single thing he'd given me, which was easy because it was just maybe two drawings and a card.

Thoughts of what happened haunted me for months. I hated thinking about him, but I always thought about him. I wanted to burn him off of my skin during too-hot showers. Everything I did seemed to be self-destructive. I was disassociating. I felt disconnected from time and reality the rest of the year.

It's probably my fault anyway. That is, if it even happened. How could it have happened? Obviously, it isn't real. None of it is. I probably just made him up, and now I'm lying to everyone. I'm just a liar.

One day a thought broke through as the hot water of the shower hit me.

If it isn't real, then why does it hurt so bad?

The reality of my situation suddenly felt like a hand gripping me, forcing me to face forward and acknowledge it.

Tyler really did fuck me up. It really did happen. I'm not fooling anyone. He did all those things to me. He hurt me that much. He made me afraid to share my opinions and true self with the people around me.

My legs guided me down to the floor of the shower. I felt so empty, like nothing. Like I could sink into the floor and never return. I slowly curled in on myself, and held my legs close to my chest. The tears wouldn't come.

~ • ~

Three months later, I realized he was still following my Spotify account, so out of panic and the realization that I couldn't block people, I made playlists with titles like "holy shit unfollow me" and "please unfollow me."

And he did. But then I saw the title of the playlist he made on his own account: "i saw you at school and almost killed myself."

I opened the playlist.

"i saw you at school. i never wanted to fucking hurt you" was the description.

I felt sick. It was the middle of the night, around four maybe. I sat crying silently in my bed, trying to convince myself that I wasn't crazy. I felt like I should've died, because it already felt like he killed me. None of this should've ever happened. I finally climbed out of bed and went into the living room where my mom was sleeping on the couch. She blinked the sleep out of her hazel green eyes, then sat up and said, "Hey, what's wrong?"

I sat next to her and cried as I told her what happened.

That fall, I switched schools. Scriber Lake High School was on the same campus as the homeschool, but it was still pretty separate. My mom and I thought I would do better somewhere away from the people I was hanging out with, especially Tyler. I was doing well, and I had received my first awards ever—a perfect attendance award from the school, and an Entry class award from my teacher, Nate. I was in high spirits as I walked out of school and hopped on my bus to go home.

The sound of at least twenty other students flooded around me as I got on the bus.

After I paid the bus driver, I turned to walk down the aisle and glanced at the faces as I passed. Then I caught a glimpse of Tyler's hair, bright oranges and pinks forming a sunset. I hadn't seen him in five months. We locked eyes, his piercing blue and pale, mine open wide. My grip loosened, and I had to adjust to keep from dropping everything. I turned back around, thoughts exploding in my head as the chatter of what felt like one thousand students kept swirling in my ears.

My stomach knotted, my insides felt cold while I was starting to sweat outside. My mind was going a mile a minute.

He might try to talk to me. What if he tries to get me back? Why today? I was having such a good day. I can't do this, I have to run. I have to get off this bus.

My fingers started to tap rhythmically against my other hand as I waited for an opening to present itself in the horde. I could hear my friend ask, faintly, "Are you okay?"

I looked at him. I tried to speak, but all I could say was "sorry" when I saw a small window of opportunity open up in the massive crowd. I ran.

"Whoa!" the bus driver said as I jumped onto the street.

My legs felt heavy. I was shaking like a dog. It was hard to breathe.

Okay, don't cry. Maybe it wasn't him? It was him. It was definitely him. He looked at me. He looked at me and he saw me. Why did he see me? I wish I was invisible.

My friends were so far away from me. I couldn't run; all I could do was walk as stiff as a board, my hand up to my face as I tried to calm down. One of my friends spotted me, and they all started to walk toward me. I was going to cry. My barrier was breaking. I was panicking.

When they reached me I said, "I saw him."

My voice was barely a whisper. I broke down sobbing on the sidewalk. I fell to my knees, and cried.

I didn't feel like I would ever get better. I didn't think I would ever heal.

I had dreams of him humiliating me, dreams of him following me, dreams of him killing me.

I started seeing a therapist that spring. I squirmed in my seat as I recalled past events with Tyler. The therapist's worried look comforted me in a way. She shook her head in bewilderment at my story.

"Yeah, everyone's saying it was abusive, but . . . I don't know. I'm probably overreacting, or faking it or something," I mumbled, laughing nervously and messing with the sleeves of my jacket.

She nodded and stood up. "Actually, that way of thinking is a textbook symptom," she said. She grabbed a book from her shelf. My stomach dropped when I saw the words "emotional" and "abuse" on the cover. Jesus, I thought I was going to throw up. I felt cold as she flipped through the pages littered with colorful tabs. Her fingers landed on a page, and I sat as still as a statue as she read the passage from the book, almost identical to the words I had just spoken. They didn't pass by my head like usual; they were slowly soaking in. The gears were moving, moving, moving. Then the gears stopped.

"Oh."

I'm not faking it.

It took a while to feel any emotion about that, but when the relief came, it was like nothing I'd ever felt before. It was such a strange mix of happiness and anguish. I finally knew what was happening to me.

~ • ~

It's still hard for me, sometimes. Recovery is anything but linear, and I have days where I fall back into negative thinking patterns, like believing it wasn't that bad. But it doesn't last as long anymore, and I'm getting closer and closer to truly believing myself and those around me. Ants, rollie pollies, and spiders are waltzing around me, and it seems we have a mutual respect for each other; they aren't crawling on me and I'm not disturbing them. I want to be this comfortable all the time. I want my mind to be this quiet. A breeze as soft as a blanket is enveloping me as I decide to compose a letter to this ghost in front of me.

> You don't have to keep trying with those friends. You don't have to keep trying with Tyler. You can let go, and I promise you, you'll be so much happier in a few years. People will come and go, and you have to let it happen. Don't blame yourself for not knowing, or "letting it go on for too long," because it's not true. When other people won't listen to you, you have to let them figure it out on their own, because you can't force them to see where you're coming from. That isn't to say you're not allowed to care; you're always allowed to care. But your life is yours alone, and their lives are theirs. Don't let them consume you.
>
> You'll be happy one day, I promise. You'll meet some genuine people, go to therapy, and you'll have a real, loving relationship. You'll go through some rough spots in life, but you'll learn to handle them better, and they'll help you. You won't bottle things up anymore. You and I both know you've done that your whole life. Life will never be perfect; it can't be, but you can live. You can breathe. You can cry. You can love, you can trust. And you'll find that that's enough. One day, you'll realize you haven't thought about something negative in two days. It gets easier. The slow days won't feel so painful, and you'll look outside and see all the beauty. You'll see the sunrise again. Not because you haven't slept, but because you're about to start the day. The birds chirping and singing around you right now are singing for you. They're mourning the kid you are now, and celebrating who you will become soon. There's hope. Don't give up.
>
> Love, Emil (P.S. We're almost 18 now! You did it!)

I never really had a chance to be myself back then. I wish I could show my ghost what I've accomplished, and what I've overcome. I think he'd be proud of me. He and his life were a stepping stone to get where I am now, and I couldn't be more grateful.

FROM THE AUTHOR

I can honestly say I'm so much happier now than I used to be. While all of this was happening, I could relate to every word of the song "Ghosting" by Mother Mother, but now only one lyric stands out: "and this is why I have decided / to leave your house and home un-haunted." I'm starting to understand my trauma, and because of that, it won't have the power to haunt me as much. I wrote this story partly to gain some clarity for myself, but also to reach out to others who've been emotionally abused—whether they know it or not. I'm hoping I succeed in both aspects. I started writing when the wound was still fresh, and the process helped me realize a lot of things. I still have bad days, but they're spread out now, and things that used to trigger and leave me panicking are more bearable. It feels good to finally have goals for the future (I want to become a baker!), and I'm becoming more comfortable expressing my emotions and opinions. Writing this was kind of terrifying because I was—and still am—scared that no one will see these events as a big deal. But I have faith that someone will read this and understand what I'm talking about. If you do understand, this story is for you. You aren't crazy. It's not your fault, and it can get better. Healing is a tricky process, but it can happen. You can do it. Don't give up.

YOUTUBE CHANNEL
STEEP STAIRS PRESS

bit.ly/3hqiUiM

Screaming Dude
Stephanie Souza
2019

CICATRIZ ROSA

Yahaira Souza

As the trees drift away, the colors start to smear past the fast-moving bus. I really did it this time: I'm holding on to what is now *my* guitar like it's my child—which I will keep safe. I name him Ladron, because he is going to steal the show when I perform! I remember what my teacher said just a few hours earlier: *"I was given two guitars by a couple in Edmonds and they told me to make sure to give them to the right people. I think you are one of them."*

I can't believe it. Of all the people, she chose me. *Well, then I must be pretty alright at being a musician if she believes in me.*

"Hey!" someone says. I snap out of my thoughts, realizing an older man across the aisle is talking to me.

"What?" I say, and my voice cracks. I'm nervous because I don't live in the safest area.

"Play me a song! Play it something like 'do-da-do-dooo-da-ra-do,'" he says as he strums an air guitar. He has wide eyes that pop with passion, like he is ready for whatever comes next. He wears a nice jean jacket, and he's mostly bald with grey patches that contrast with his ebony skin.

I look around the bus to see who else is listening; I have to make sure I'm not just seeing things. I'm confused and nervous, but down to talk.

"I wish I could, but I have a long ride home. I can't get kicked off the bus," I say.

"How about something like 'do-ra-do-deee-dooo?'" he asks with a jazzy voice. I chuckle lightheartedly, but I'm not sure what to do. *Do I start playing?*

"Sorry, but I can't. There's too many people," I tell him.

"Let me tell you something. Do you see signs that say you can't play an instrument?"

"Well, there is one that says you can't play music," I answer.

"But not anything about instruments!" he says joyfully. "See, at one time there were signs that said black people couldn't sit on a certain side of the bus. It was a rule. Did it *make* it wrong or was it *truly* wrong?" His eye twitches a little, like he has seen things and has stories to tell. Lucky me—I have the chance to listen.

"Now look at me! I can sit where I want!" he gleams. "Music is a beautiful thing that deserves to be shared with the world and people around you. Don't ever let anyone take it away from you! Ever!"

I know he's right, but I'm not sure what to do. "I don't have enough room here, but I can play once we get off the bus," I say.

I turn to watch all of the scenery, houses, and streets slip past my window. Suddenly the brakes screech and we are at the transit center, my stop. I grab the guitar, swing my backpack on, and head off the bus.

The sun is soon to set, but for now it's still hesitant. Switching through the chords I know, I start to play a little tune, and he dances behind me, with a little pep in his step.

When I finish the song, he pants a little and we burst into laughter.

"Straight from the soul!" he says. He points at me, then walks away.

Even though people watch as if we're from another planet, I don't care. I'm enjoying a moment where everything feels like it has fallen into place in the world.

This moment is real. I know I'm here. I can't say the same for many other days during this past decade where I seemed to constantly lose touch with who I was—and question what was real and what wasn't.

~ • ~

"I'm leaving," I said to my brother. I reached for my sweater and shoes in a hurry to escape through the door.

"No, you're not. It's too dark. You'll get kidnapped," he said. His brows wrinkled and his eyes were like that of a panther, narrowed with frustration and disapproval.

"I can't stand the yelling. I'm not feeling well. I need to go," I said. I couldn't block the sounds in the background. I didn't know how it began, but I knew I wasn't about to get into it. Some days I'd walk to the gas station when the stars were out and the moon was glistening and buy myself store-brand chocolate. Coming home, I'd tuck myself into bed and turn the music on and the dams would break. Tears would drench my cheeks. I'd feel my heart crack and it'd hurt like hell. Chocolate felt like the sweetest thing in my life.

"If you go, I'm coming," he said.

He followed me out of our Lynnwood apartment. I was already feeling refreshed. At night, things never felt as real as they did during the day. The fall air was crisp and reminded me of the nights I did a paper route with my older sister. We would be buried in stacks of newspapers from sundown to sunrise, blasting music and drinking Jack in the Box coffee to stay awake. The pay was shit, but hard work pays less sometimes.

When we got to a tunnel my brother pulled out a blunt.

"This is top-shelf," he said.

"Nice."

I sat on the curb, spacing out at the spray-painted walls as he lit up the blunt.

People told me weed could make everything better. Panic attacks since I was five, depression, bipolar disorder, hallucinations. It was supposed to be great for those kinds of things.

But the psychedelic feelings were not enough for me to want to go back home with all of the arguments. It was depressing. It seemed like no one really wanted to be there. We all had the same routine: go to school/work, come home, eat, watch TV or look at our phones, sleep. It wasn't living; it was just time wasting away. I didn't want things to be like that forever, and I definitely wanted better things for my younger brother and nephew.

By the age of 15 I was already used to the depression. All of the things in my life I couldn't control had created a monster that hung over my shoulders—a monster who was very kind when you got to know him. He was just as sad as I was, and the thought of suicide was comfortable for him too.

As we continued walking down the street, my brother started playing Gorillaz' "Feel Good Inc." on his phone. I had to buckle up, because my heart began to palpitate as loud as a bass drum and faster than a rocket ship. When I looked over at him, his face transformed into bats, screeching and flapping their wings into the night stars. I heard the blood in my ears racing briskly through my veins. I couldn't breathe. When I looked at him again, his face was normal.

"What's wrong?" my brother asked with wide eyes when he saw the terror on my face.

"I don't feel so good," I said. "My heart feels like it's gonna explode." I pointed to my throat, and he looked over to see it trying to beat through my chest. In my head, I was holding my heart in my hand.

I had been having hallucinations for about two years, and they always happened the same way. One day I'd been looking through my phone when I glanced up and heard the crunch of bones: it was me, suspended in the air with a broken spine. I had been treated at Seattle Children's Hospital twice—once for three days, diagnosis: bipolar disorder; the other time for five days, diagnosis: schizoaffective disorder.

"Holy shit," my brother said, grabbing his head and pulling his hair. His paranoia was deep regarding my regular chest pain, but he hadn't seen me like this before. "Call an ambulance!" he said.

He ran, leaving me alone on the sidewalk. He had to get rid of the weed; he didn't want to get involved with the police.

Somehow, I dialed 911, then waited for what felt like forever for an ambulance to arrive. Two paramedics got out and came over to where I stood.

"I don't know what's going on. I think it's a panic attack," I told them.

One of them laughed and said, "Breathe."

His laugh invalidated everything. *How do you know what I'm feeling or what it's like?*

"But my heart is racing and I don't know what to do. I'm scared," I said.

They asked a series of questions, and I tried to answer them. Finally, I got into the ambulance and they told me to get on the stretcher.

As I looked at my reflection in the window from within the ambulance, I wasn't sure if I was human. I repeated my name in my head, *Yahaira, Yahaira,* so I wouldn't forget. As I repeated it, though, it lost its meaning. Like I was going to forget anyway.

When we arrived at the hospital, flames engulfed my room. The walls were melting to the very ground, and the mirror was moving in circles with my heart still jumping in my chest. *Hell is going to take me tonight.*

Death had always drawn my attention. Since I was a kid, my grandma told me about a paradise that was beyond my circumstance: heaven. A place without pain, with all you could ever dream of. I wanted to go there. I wanted to escape our two-bedroom apartment where nine of us slept on the floor with blankets. People I knew living in the same area began to move to nice houses and it felt like the rapture. They were lifted to a good life, but it wasn't my family's time yet. I asked my grandma why we couldn't get to heaven sooner.

"Suicide is a sin and you'll go to hell if you try," she told me once, with a look of concern. She seemed uncertain—despite her faith in religion—about what might come after.

As the IV monitor hummed, I stared at my shoes, trying to regain my sanity.

You're human. You're seeing flames because of something happening in your head.

My heart kept kicking and punching, trying its best to escape the wall of meat and bones within. It seemed like there could be a bloody mess in seconds. "Please, please don't run away from me," I told it.

The nurse walked in with a smile on her face, like this was just some kind of joke to everyone. *I might as well die, save myself the shame.*

She stuck a needle in my arm. "It's gonna be a little cold," she said with a grin.

The cool liquid poured through every vein and spread to my chest as she connected me to the IV. I took a deep breath, hoping it would end. For a moment my brain thought I was drowning, but it didn't matter to me.

I tried my best to rest on that hospital bed as time ticked over my head, but life went by in slow motion.

This is it, I'm leaving tonight.

"You'll be alright?" the nurse asked. I nodded. She laughed again then left.

I struggled to keep my eyes open, like they were made of stone and everything was trying to go black.

"You can close your eyes now."

The voice was a whisper, soothing and soft. There was someone or something next to me, and his words slithered into my ears like snakes. His shadow was comforting, but his whispers sent shivers that spread from my ears to the rest of my body.

"Come with me and I'll make you a promise. You'll never hurt again."

He sounded convincing. What could he be? A demon? The devil? An angel?

Whatever he was, his voice seemed like a bright light that could pull me to somewhere safe. My eyes darted around as he spoke, as if he could read my thoughts. Every time I closed my eyes, my blood pressure dropped and my eyes shot up regardless of how heavy they were or how tired I was.

"I'm trying to go with you . . . but I think you're the devil," I said to him.

"I'm not gonna hurt you."

"You know I don't want to stay . . . but I can't trust you."

With that, he vanished.

My heart sank. *Wait . . . maybe I made a mistake.*

~ • ~

A few months of jumping from medication to medication wore me out. Nothing seemed to work, and the side effects were pretty intense. One was like a poke in my head that gave me the urge to eat like I was starving. Not even the paralyzing paranoia was as bad as the urge to stuff myself. I tried really hard to believe that I was getting closer to being stable again, but I kept having to return to the psychiatrist to adjust the meds. All I wanted was to pull myself out of the other dimensions I visited.

~ • ~

One day my sisters, my brother, my nephew, and I were on our way to see *Avengers: Endgame*, but we had to stop at Fred Meyer first to get my medication. I had been too anxious to ask anyone in my family to drive me to get it the day before, so it had been over 24 hours since I'd taken anything.

I didn't take it because I wanted to feel more than I had in awhile; I didn't want to be protected by the atmosphere that thickened around me. I wanted to peel the skin off and see the bare reality, revealing the tender pink freakiness in everything. The world was inside out and the people were, too. This was a place where it was easy for the voices to reach me; it was inspiring and chilling, my second dimension.

With all of the raw emotions, the taste of blood lingered in the air and on my tongue. I didn't question, just accepted. The world had a touch of red, like danger, like *this isn't where I should be but I thought I would like it here.*

We pulled into the parking lot and stopped in front of the store.

The lyrics to "Song for CA" by Field Trip streamed through my headphones and blew kisses at me, but I didn't want them.

"It wasn't easy honey, you were the one I loved most."

"Hurry up, we're gonna miss the movie," my sister said, noticeably annoyed.

Hands had sprouted from the seat, holding me down. I couldn't move. I sat, unresponsive and drained of energy. My soul tugged at me to go toward the sunset, but it wasn't my time. There was nothing to hold my ever-drifting mind, no meds to ease the punches of certain realities.

"Come on," she said. "I wanna make it on time."

Maybe I'll feel normal like I did before. Maybe I can watch a movie at the theater without the meds. I'm just not gonna take them.

I made up my mind and dragged myself out of the car. I felt my eyes droop like a bloodhound while walking toward the pharmacy. I felt the breeze blowing through my bones. Eyes began to peer all over the place.

The sun was out, but the day felt gloomy.

"Here to pick up some medicine?" the lady behind the pharmacy counter said in a friendly tone.

"Yup."

I wasn't feeling up to smiling. *Guess it is not so bad if I let my mood get the best of me this once.* Walking out, the fresh scent of flowers smacked my face. I stopped to admire them. *They're too pretty to look at and not feel better, right?* Flowers in different colors, all fresh and nicely put together, with a sweet scent.

But my eyes began to sting. I felt empty and small like everything was about to collapse. I was trying to comfort myself, but still, my cheeks became a waterpark of tears. *Will there ever be someone to hand me some pretty little flowers, picked from a random garden?*

I'll never be able to walk the earth as others do. Never be normal with a clean mind.

~ • ~

"Does anyone have any questions?" the psychiatric unit teacher asked. I raised my hand.

"I hear my heart beating," I said. I felt the blood pump and gush into my veins, through my hands. Tired and heavy. It was the new medicine. Lithium to treat the bipolar. Every minute felt like an hour and every hour felt like three.

"I get pretty hyper-aware, too, sometimes," she said. I knew she was trying to understand, but she just didn't get it.

Things felt bleak, bland, and tasteless. That seemed to be the point sometimes. Out the window was a building with tinted windows that blocked anything worth seeing. Hallways and simple offices—it was all claustrophobic. Waiting for the next class, history, or whatever. It didn't help much to tell me things I already knew about coping mechanisms; it was frustrating and repetitive.

All I wanted to do was leave. I spent hours looking out the window waiting for my mom because she told me she'd visit every day. She would bring me my favorite drink: a triple chocolate Frappuccino. I felt guilty putting her through this—her time was valuable and work was important to her. We had been living paycheck to paycheck since I was born.

When my grandparents lived with us, the nine of us were crammed into a two-bedroom apartment. I remember it all vividly: my grandma happy and dancing, but also tears rolling down her cheeks as she listened to music for the heartbroken. Or moments where I walked into my aunt's room and she would light something on fire and toss it in the trash just to watch it burn. I appreciated the moments where sadness or boredom would be disrupted by Mexican music. We would dance everything away.

"*Baila para que se te quite lo triste,*" my grandma would say. "*Si te sientes enojada, no más pon música y ponte a bailar.*"

When my grandpa came home, he would dance, too. My grandma and grandpa made my heart whole. No matter what.

At school, I didn't have many friends. I didn't have the motivation to talk much, and I always went back to being alone at lunch or recess. I felt safer that way. Loneliness was captivating.

At the end of the day, I felt happy because I had my grandma at home. At one point she insisted I go and get checked to see if everything was alright in my head. There was hope that it was just a phase and I would be fine.

Then came the day when they had to leave for Mexico.

How to dance without them? And all of the food that gave color and culture to my family? They packed it in their bags when they left.

The music, the pictures, the spark that this family had: gone. Things felt hollow for a while. I had never met my dad, and, as much as I loved my mom, I realized at one point that I didn't know her like I knew other people. I realized this at nine years old, so I asked her what her favorite colors were.

"Black and red."

They became my favorite colors, too.

Every time my mom had to leave the hospital, I hugged her tight until one of the medics directed me back to class.

The darkness seemed inescapable.

~ • ~

I'm surprised when my bus arrives just in time. I step up, tap my bus pass, and take a seat. Looking out the window, I see the dancing man wander off and I realize this probably wasn't his stop. And then I wonder, *Will he still be real when I turn around?*

When the bus takes off he vanishes into the crowd. The transit center disappears into the world and the sunset caves into the blue. With the story of this moment closed, what will become of him?

What will become of me later today, tomorrow, or even in the years to come?

I look down at the guitar in my hands and think, *I just want to make it all worthwhile.*

for EVERYONE else

FROM THE AUTHOR

Since writing this story, I have found the right medications for me. I finally feel comfortable in my head and with myself after a long period of believing that medications would only alter my personality. My psychiatrist made adjustments after hearing about the negative effects. I find I'm still the same person, just without the symptoms.

I started college in the middle of the pandemic, and I'm learning how to get by. My dreams are all about becoming a successful musician; my goal is to finish the projects I've begun in order to release them! Another goal is to gain experience as a tattoo artist, or to start a business selling my own clothing line.

I chose to write my story because I hadn't seen anything like it in books or movies before. The only stories I see are about how others live with people like me, usually portrayed as people to avoid. My story is simply a glimpse into what it's like. I plan to use my unique experiences to my advantage, and I want to motivate others to do the same. I want to leave readers feeling a little more aware of schizoaffective disorder. I want those with mental illnesses to feel like they have one more story to connect with, to hold onto the good moments while they pull through the bad—even if they feel like the bad has lasted for years. Things will get better; it just takes time.

"What if the dice have been rolled and conditions change?"
—Ahmed Sheba, "Alla Kushnir Dancer"

YOUTUBE CHANNEL
STEEP STAIRS PRESS

bit.ly/3hqiUiM

RESOURCES

INTRODUCTION TO THE
STEEP STAIRS PODCAST

Chelsi Gorzelsky

I work at an organization in Seattle called foundry10. We seek to expand the way people think about learning, and we do that by partnering with open-minded, innovative thinkers at non-traditional schools like Scriber Lake High School. Toward the end of 2019, I met with a few educators who were interested in bringing audio tools into their non-audio classrooms in a variety of ways. That's when I met Marjie, and we clicked right away.

In January 2020, Marjie and I made plans for a pilot of a unique English class which would incorporate digital audio to enhance student learning. This collaboration between Scriber and foundry10 was going well! We decided we would read *On the Come Up* by Angie Thomas, a story about a young woman trying to make it as a musician. We talked about the book together and helped students create their own poetry and music in response to what they were reading and discussing. With only a few weeks left in the quarter, I brought in an audio kit and a group of students gravitated towards the equipment immediately. They sat together around a single table, having entire conversations through the mics and headphones. "Do you think we could make a podcast in this class?" they asked. Of course we could! Marjie and I planned our final project: a podcast episode where students would interview each other, role-play as characters from the book, and share the music and poetry they created in response to Thomas' literature.

And then the state locked down. We tumbled into uncertainty and scrambled to figure out how we were going to serve our students. Rachel Ramey, Scriber's librarian, suggested we try using a podcast to connect students facing remote learning for the first time. Fortunately, we had a group of podcast visionaries ready to take this journey with us! In those early pandemic days, we figured it out together, and our brave group of students produced "Scriber Under Quarantine," our very first episode. Our pilot proved successful in a way we never imagined it would! Marjie, Rachel, and I looked ahead to Fall 2020 and prepared for a fully virtual school year launch. With a completely new group of students (our original podcasters had all graduated), we continued to explore topics important to youth and wove their experiences together with stories written by authors in the Steep Stairs writing program. Students in our classes connected with past Steep Stairs authors through our exploration and were inspired to contribute their own voices along the way. (See more about this endeavor in "The Stories that Youth Uncover Under Quarantine," an article on the foundry10 Medium website.)

I asked our podcast visionaries, "How do you want to share these stories and podcasts? Who do you want to share them with?" They responded, "With everyone, as far as we can reach. We want everyone to hear our stories."

To hear their stories and full Steep Stairs Podcast episodes, use the QR code or corresponding link below to visit the Steep Stairs Press YouTube channel. Check back often as more content is added. Thanks for listening!

bit.ly/3hqiUiM

YOUTUBE CHANNEL
STEEP STAIRS PRESS

for EVERYONE else

BIBLIOTHERAPY AND THE SCRIBER BOOKS, UPDATED

Leighanne Law and Rachel Ramey

The stories in the Scriber books speak directly to students' lived experiences, giving voice and validation to what they once presumed should be silenced and shamed. With authenticity and radical acceptance, these stories grapple with mental health, gender identity and expression, family dynamics, issues around immigration, sexual abuse, grieving, and addiction. They are always the first prescription for bibliotherapy—the practice of using books to heal.

But what do you recommend to someone who has read every Scriber book and is clamoring for more? How do you keep the fire fueled? You can start with the following go-to list of further reading, organized by theme:

PROCESSING DEATH OR LOSS
- *They Both Die at the End*, Adam Silvera
- *We Are Okay*, Nina LaCour
- *The Hate U Give*, Angie Thomas
- *The Beauty that Remains*, Ashley Woodfolk
- *Essential Maps for the Lost*, Deb Caletti
- *The Boy in the Black Suit*, Jason Reynolds
- *Long Way Down*, Jason Reynolds
- *Bearing the Unbearable*, Joanne Cacciatore
- *Kids of Appetite*, David Arnold
- *Some Kind of Courage*, Dan Gemeinhart
- *Life in a Fishbowl*, Len Vlahos
- *Dancing at the Pity Party*, Tyler Feder

ADDICTION
- *Tweak*, Nic Sheff
- *We All Fall Down*, Nic Sheff
- *The Crank Trilogy* (*Crank*, *Glass*, and *Fallout*), Ellen Hopkins
- *Forged by Fire*, Sharon M. Draper
- *Beneath a Meth Moon*, Jacqueline Woodson
- *Gabi, a Girl in Pieces*, Isabel Quintero
- *Rodent*, Lisa J. Lawrence
- *Finding Hope*, Colleen Nelson
- *This Is the Part Where You Laugh*, Peter Brown Hoffmeister
- *The Way Back*, Carrie Mac

SEXUAL ABUSE AND ASSAULT
- *A + E 4Ever*, Ilike Merey
- *The Gospel of Winter*, Brendan Kiely
- *Exit, Pursued by a Bear*, E. K. Johnston
- *Speak*, Laurie Halse Anderson
- *Hunger*, Roxane Gay
- *The Female of the Species*, Mindy McGinnis
- *Asking for It*, Louise O'Neill
- *Jaya and Rasa*, Sonia Patel
- *Take It as a Compliment*, Maria Stoian
- *I Have the Right To*, Chessy Prout
- *Moxie*, Jennifer Mathieu
- *Saints and Misfits*, S. K. Ali
- *The Music of What Happens*, Bill Konigsberg

GENDER EXPRESSION AND IDENTITY
- *Every Day*, David Levithan
- *When the Moon Was Ours*, Anna-Marie McLemore
- *Symptoms of Being Human*, Jeff Garvin
- *The Body Is Not an Apology*, Sonya Renee Taylor
- *And She Was*, Jessica Verdi
- *Freakboy*, Kristin Elizabeth Clark
- *Gender Outlaw*, Kate Bornstein
- *Parrotfish*, Ellen Wittlinger

- *Love Beyond Body, Space, and Time*, Hope Nicholson
- *Beyond Magenta*, Susan Kuklin
- *The Gender Quest Workbook*, Rylan Jay Testa et al.
- *The Prince and the Dressmaker*, Jen Wang
- *The 57 Bus*, Dashka Slater
- *Check, Please!*, Ngozi Ukazu
- *Felix Ever After*, Kacen Callender
- *Girl Mans Up*, M-E Girard
- *Laura Dean Keeps Breaking Up with Me*, Mariko Tamaki
- *I Wish You All the Best*, Mason Deaver
- *All Boys Aren't Blue*, George M. Johnson

FAMILY DYNAMICS
- *Between the World and Me*, Ta-Nehisi Coates
- *Fun Home*, Alison Bechdel
- *Are You My Mother?*, Alison Bechdel
- *Hey, Kiddo*, Jarrett J. Krosoczka
- *Everything I Never Told You*, Celeste Ng
- *When Dimple Met Rishi*, Sandhya Menon
- *Losers Bracket*, Chris Crutcher
- *I Am Not Your Perfect Mexican Daughter*, Erica L. Sánchez
- *Blood Family*, Anne Fine
- *Fire Color One*, Jenny Valentine
- *The Memory Trees*, Kali Wallace
- *Same Family, Different Colors*, Lori L. Tharps
- *The Education of Margot Sanchez*, Lilliam Rivera
- *The Agony of Bun O'Keefe*, Heather Smith
- *Long Live the Tribe of Fatherless Girls*, T Kira Madden

IMMIGRATION
- *In the Country We Love*, Diane Guerrero
- *The Distance Between Us*, Reyna Grande
- *Americanized*, Sara Saedi
- *An Indigenous Peoples' History of the United States*,
  Roxanne Dunbar-Ortiz
- *This Land Is Our Land*, Linda Barrett Osborne

- *American Street*, Ibi Zoboi
- *Enrique's Journey*, Sonia Nazario
- *Saint Death*, Marcus Sedgwick
- *Tell Me How It Ends*, Valeria Luiselli
- *The Line Becomes a River*, Francisco Cantú
- *Born a Crime*, Trevor Noah
- *A Girl Like That*, Tanaz Bhathena
- *The Poet X*, Elizabeth Acevedo

MENTAL HEALTH
- *The Body Keeps the Score*, Bessel van der Kolk
- *The Art of Feeling*, Laura Tims
- *Suicide Notes*, Michael Thomas Ford
- *Challenger Deep*, Neal Shusterman
- *The Memory of Light*, Francisco X. Stork
- *Eating Mindfully*, Susan Albers
- *Madness*, Zac Brewer
- *Turtles All the Way Down*, John Green
- *Highly Illogical Behavior*, John Corey Whaley
- *The Rest of Us Just Live Here*, Patrick Ness
- *Six of Crows*, Leigh Bardugo
- *Fans of the Impossible Life*, Kate Scelsa
- *Darius the Great Is Not Okay*, Adib Khorram
- *The Astonishing Color of After*, Emily X. R. Pan
- *How to Make Friends with the Dark*, Kathleen Glasgow
- *Eliza and Her Monsters*, Francesca Zappia

for EVERYONE else

IN MEMORIAM

Bob and Mele Fuller

OUR KIDS:
BOB FULLER'S INVESTMENT

Marjie Bowker

Bob Fuller had the gift of seeing promise in young people. Four years before he passed away, he proposed a plan that would alter the lives of three Scriber Lake High School students.

Kelly Peterson was one of them.

Kelly checked herself into rehab at the age of 18, two years before her life intersected with Bob's. At that point her future felt distant and false. She was sure she was dying. She didn't want to keep drinking, but without alcohol life was something she didn't think she could handle.

She bought a Hello Kitty notebook to keep track of the details. If she came out on the other side, she knew writing about it might help others in the same situation. She had done this once before, while she was a student at Scriber Lake.

Since 2011, over 120 students like Kelly have faced issues such as addiction, abuse, neglect, depression, and bullying through writing and publishing their stories.

As a sophomore, Kelly had written about a terrifying event involving drugs. Even though publishing it was an empowering experience, her struggles continued. Entering rehab, she intended to write even more honestly. Her life seemed to depend on it.

Kelly was a year clean when she used the details in her notebook to write "Stepping from Oblivion" as a veteran for Scriber's fifth book, *I'm Finally Awake*.

Bob Fuller came to that book release event in the spring of 2016, and—as usual—lingered to greet all of the authors and to commend them for their courage and determination. He also mentioned he had an idea he wanted to run by me.

Bob had been an enthusiastic supporter of Scriber's writing program—and of me as its founder—since the beginning. He came to every event: the book releases, the readings, and the plays we staged with Seattle Public Theater bringing these stories to life. He would send me encouraging emails afterwards with helpful insights and observations. Every year he would donate a substantial amount to help with publishing costs, and he would schedule our student authors to speak at Lynnwood Rotary lunch meetings.

Bob already did so much, I couldn't imagine what else he had in mind. A few weeks after the book release, he and his wife, Mele, presented me with a document outlining their idea: they wanted to provide postsecondary school funding for one student per year.

They also wanted me to choose the student—one of the published authors. They would make tuition payments directly to the school of that student's choice. No strings attached. No grade minimum. Their support would continue through graduation, and they wanted no recognition whatsoever. They just wanted to invest in the future of kids who demonstrated so much growth and drive.

Many community members have supported Scriber students in thoughtful and generous ways, and staff members often act as the conduit for those gestures. We shower our students with love, both in school and beyond. We ask them about their dreams and encourage development of their strengths, skills, and talents. But when they leave our network of support by graduation or choice, life happens. Financial troubles and myriad obstacles get in the way of dreams. This is when young people—especially those who have experienced trauma—need people who will continue to walk with them through the hard stuff.

The Fullers understood this.

When I chose Kelly that first year, Bob and Mele committed to supporting her dream of becoming a teacher. They adopted Shea Ensz the next year, and Santino Dewyer the year after that. The Fullers removed financial obstacles for each of them, personalizing their support according to each situation. They covered tuition payments, living expenses, books, and even some necessary household items. They sent birthday money and gifts, met for coffee, attended presentations and graduations, and invited all of us over for multiple Mele-cooked dinners. Bob, Mele, and I called them "our kids."

Our kids put this support to work. Kelly holds a master's degree in education, and she is a special education teacher in the Lake Washington School District. Shea has completed three years at Evergreen State College. And Santino is preparing to enter the Park Ranger Law Enforcement Academy at Skagit Valley College.

Although Bob had survived several earlier bouts of lung cancer, we learned in the spring of 2020 that his cancer had metastasized in the form of a brain tumor. While undergoing cancer treatments months before his death, Bob informed me of an account he created through the Rotary to continue paying expenses for the kids. That account is active today.

My heart sinks every time I think of all the kids who will never experience the unconditional, hands-on support Bob provided. However, when I think of the young lives he has changed forever, my heart soars. I have seen and felt the transformative effect of his care and generosity. Bob figured out how to find happiness through giving to others, and he gave me a front row seat to witness all of it.

~ • ~

Mele granted permission to tell this story in honor of Bob and his extraordinary commitment. See their adoptees' stories on the following pages.

KELLY PETERSON
"Take A Bow" • *You've Got It All Wrong* (2013)
"Stepping From Oblivion" • *I'm Finally Awake* (2016)

I was nervous when I first met the Fullers. No one in my life had ever offered me such an incredible opportunity. In fact, I wasn't sure if it was true, or if I could even trust such an offer. I had little to no experience with the altruistic behavior of others, and I had no idea how much my life would change as a result of their kindness. It was indescribable. The things they did for me far surpassed their initial offer: in addition to tuition, they invited me over to their home and made food on multiple occasions, taking care to accommodate my dietary needs. During my student teaching, they helped with my living costs. They sent me a microwave after I mentioned I didn't have one. When I finished school, Bob cut his family trip to Washington DC short to fly back and attend my graduation ceremony. Their support absolutely changed my life. Now that I'm a teacher, many more students will benefit from their generosity. I hope to support someone in a similar way as soon as possible.

SHEA ENSZ
"They" • *I'm Finally Awake* (2016)

The first time I met the Fullers was at their house for dinner, and Mele made the best vegan enchiladas I have ever tasted. Bob and Mele showed Kelly and me around their home in downtown Edmonds, from their garden full of berries and flowers to the beautiful view of the Puget Sound from their front deck. I still have not forgotten the relief and excitement I felt the moment they handed me the paperwork outlining their scholarship offer after we finished the homemade berry crumble Mele made for dessert.

It is because of the Fullers that I was able to attend Evergreen State College, my college of choice, for three years, something I never saw in my future because of financial issues. Mele and Bob granted me the opportunity to seek higher education in my dream field of study, and because of their offer, I had the best times of my life attending college. The experiences they gifted me have been fulfilling beyond what I ever imagined I would be allowed.

During my freshman year at Evergreen, when my dinosaur of a laptop I had been using for all my classes finally died for good, they bought me a brand-new laptop and added some extra spending money for warm clothes for the winter season. They visited me during the science carnival and showed support during my presentation. After I moved out of the dorms, they aided me with my living costs, including a portion of my rent and medical bills, which allowed me to continue my independent life in Olympia while I attended college. I could never thank them enough for the scholarship, the financial assistance, and the intangible gifts I received through their generosity. Bob and Mele continue to inspire me to help those in need, and to use what I have been granted to continue the cycle of gift-giving they initiated.

SANTINO DEWYER
"Broken Promises" • *We Hope You Rise Up* (2015)

The first time I met Bob and Mele and told them about my goal of becoming a park ranger—I remember it very clearly—Bob put a hand up and said, "Don't worry about it. We will cover it. Tuition, everything. Anything you need, just let us know. We enjoy seeing young people pursue their goals and accomplish them."

Wait. Did that just happen?

Not even my parents had ever tried to push me to accomplish anything like that, so for strangers to take that on—it was very touching. And very shocking, too. But I left feeling really good knowing that I had them in my corner, ready to back me up.

Their support turned out to be much more than just financial. Bob and I met for coffee a bunch of times and just talked. I had a lot of obstacles to work through at that time, which kept me from going to school right away. So I would be frustrated or kind of angry a lot, and he would talk me through all of the situations in my life. It was more like meeting with a friend rather than with somebody who had offered to help pay for school. He really cared. He was one of those friends that always went out of his way for me and never expected anything back.

He would always say, "It's okay, I believe you can do it." He helped me look at everything in a more positive way, and made me excited for my future. When I was going through my hardships, I just kept saying to myself, *Hey, I'm going to get this done someday. I'm going to do it for Bob, for myself, and for my family.* He gave me motivation.

Hearing that Bob passed a few weeks into the pandemic was heartbreaking. He was a very good friend and I miss him. I'm finally ready to go to school—which is what we had talked about for two years—and he left me money to cover it. I'm going to make him proud; his efforts are not going to go to waste. He changed my life. Wherever he is up there, I hope he is looking down and knows that I am doing it.

Best wishes to his family; I know they miss him, too.

for EVERYONE else

George Murray

STRAIGHT TALK TO FATHERS: GEORGE MURRAY'S LEGACY

Marjie Bowker

Each fall and spring for the past nine years, George Murray invited me and two Scriber writers to the Kiwanis' Tuesday meetings at the Pancake Haus in Edmonds. He welcomed our students like ambassadors each time, encouraging them to order "anything they wanted" off the menu. (He told those who ordered pancakes to "get the big stack.") Stories were read after brunch and business, and George always followed with comments and questions. He would highlight unique resiliencies, encourage talents, and ask about future dreams. At one meeting George led the club in a request for a writer to read a rap she had woven into her story. "Rap! Rap! Rap!" the club chanted. The rapper beamed at the invitation and delivered. Another student was offered landscaping jobs, and another sold art to real customers for the first time.

George knew how to make teenagers feel seen.

I first met George in the fall of 2012. He waited outside my classroom one afternoon until the final bell rang, came around the corner using a cane, introduced himself, and told me he had read our first published book of student stories, *We Are Absolutely Not Okay*. "The Edmonds Kiwanis want to support this program any way we can," he said. He told me he recognized the heart and soul involved in helping kids write past the abuse, addiction, and abandonment in their pasts, and that he and his club wanted to be a part of moving them toward brighter futures.

George followed through with much more than the lunch invitations. He purchased classroom sets of our books and delivered them to each district high school library because he felt "all kids need to hear these stories." He showed up for readings and theater performances.

A career businessman, George was passionate about education reform and often mentioned he thought Scriber was "moving in the right direction" with our focus on storytelling and the "whole child." At a meeting in May 2017, during a time his doctors were trying to figure out what to do about his failing lungs and suggesting hospice care, George maintained his focus on what schools should be doing. He held up a book titled *Finnish Lessons 2.0: What Can the World Learn from Educational Change in Finland?* "Educational equity is the answer," he told everyone, "not the competition model we follow here. More schools need to hear this message. We need to support what Scriber is doing."

George stayed with us for almost four years past that hospice suggestion. During the last year of his life, short on oxygen and energy, George organized a Scriber chess club. On many Tuesday afternoons I would peak into their meeting room to see students sitting across from George and other Kiwanis members pondering chess moves next to a table full of pizza.

He always figured out ways to make the right things happen—things no one else would ever think about.

Through this rare brand of thoughtfulness George helped many of our students see themselves as contributors to something bigger than themselves; he also believed our kids acted as important messengers to the community. To the end, he continued to tell everyone who would listen that the Scriber books were "straight talk to fathers." He felt the stories worked as "mirrors to hold up to see how we are doing as parents."

He saw the exchange with the community as profound, equal, and interconnected, and he saw himself as the cheerleader for all of it.

Thank you, George Murray. You have left a legacy at our school.

for EVERYONE else

ACKNOWLEDGMENTS

We owe a debt of gratitude to our Edmonds community for its support this past decade. We are lucky to live in such a compassionate "village" where so many individuals take a special interest in our kids on a daily basis. Here are some highlights:

Within a year of our first publication in 2012, three men we eventually came to refer to as "The Three Musketeers" emerged as champions of our writing program: Rock Roth of the Edmonds Daybreakers Rotary, Bob Fuller of the Lynnwood Rotary, and George Murray of the Edmonds Kiwanis.

Rock passed away in 2014, and this year we lost both Bob and George. We feel these losses deeply, and we dedicate this year's book to Bob and George in recognition of their unique gifts to us. We appreciate how each man's respective club has stepped in to support us in their absence.

We have been gifted with many unexpected community partners over the years. Cal Crow (Center for Learning Connections, Edmonds College) led us to understand the research on resilience and self-efficacy in 2012. Seattle Public Theater partnered with us on the stage beginning in 2013. Trudy Catterfeld taught us how to become professional publishers in 2016. And Scarlet Parke and Dimiter Yordanov brought music to our stories in 2018.

This year, Chelsi Gorzelsky led us into the podcast world through the foundry10 organization, and Tim Holsopple took over all publishing responsibilities: the copyediting, the cover design, the interior layout, the production . . . everything! And the Edmonds Lutheran Church won't stop finding generous ways to demonstrate creative, consistent support. We are in awe of how each gift deepens and expands our program.

The Edmonds School District maintains its support in all ways, with special thanks to Superintendent Gustavo Balderas and Scriber Principal Andrea Hillman for their compassionate leadership.

Our greatest thanks, however, go to the Scriber writers' parents, who show so much courage in supporting their children.

We are grateful.

ABOUT THE EDITORS

 **MARJIE BOWKER** has taught English and a little history somewhere in the world (including China, Norway, and Vietnam) for the past 23 years, in addition to her "regular" spot at Scriber. She is a cofounder of Steep Stairs Press and is the author of two curriculum guides, *They Absolutely Want to Write: Teaching the Heart and Soul of Narrative Writing* and *Hippie Boy Teaching Guide: Transforming Lives through Personal Storytelling*, and a book based on the concepts of Appreciative Inquiry, *Creating a Success Culture: Transforming Our Schools One Question at a Time.*

 **LEIGHANNE LAW** earned her BA in English from Carleton College in Minnesota and her MA in Teaching (with a library endorsement) from the University of Washington. She has used her degrees to build a career out of reading and talking about books. After many years working as a bookseller and event coordinator, she realized that the best part of her job was connecting youth to the glorious world of reading. So, in 2014, she became Scriber's librarian. In 2019, she became the library coordinator for the Edmonds School District. She is honored to continue working with Scriber's community of storytellers.

ABOUT SCRIBER LAKE HIGH SCHOOL

Scriber Lake High is a public school of approximately 200 students in the Edmonds School District, located just north of Seattle. We are one of Washington's oldest alternative schools. Scriber is a school of choice; some students come to us as freshmen, and some come seeking a second, third, or fourth chance to graduate. A majority of our students have struggled with depression, anxiety, abuse, loss, homelessness, or drugs and alcohol, and have been lost in the educational system because of these outside factors.

In 2012, our staff accepted a three-year challenge to increase our students' sense of self-efficacy and resiliency through the use of Appreciative Inquiry questioning techniques. Under the leadership of Dr. Cal Crow, Director of the Center for Efficacy and Resiliency, we challenged ourselves to create a school filled with heart and soul—a school focused on supporting students' stories and dreams for the future.

In 2015, we published a book about our journey called *Creating a Success Culture: Transforming Our Schools One Question at a Time*. It features anecdotal stories of how we changed conversations with our students to bring them back into the center of their own education. Our book is available on Amazon, and we invite conversations with other schools working to address the needs of students impacted by childhood trauma.

CPSIA information can be obtained
at www.ICGtesting.com
Printed in the USA
FSHW021812110621

9 780997 472431